SOCIOLOGY OF LAW AND LEGAL ANTHROPOLOGY IN DUTCH-SPEAKING COUNTRIES

NIJHOFF LAW SPECIALS

D. Campbell, Abortion Law and Public Policy. 1984.
ISBN 90-247-3107-0.

J. Pictet, Development and Principles of International Humanitarian
Law. 1985.
ISBN 90-247-3199-2.

J. Van Houtte, Sociology of Law and Legal Anthropology in Dutch-
speaking Countries. 1985.
ISBN 90-247-3175-5.

Sociology of Law and Legal Anthropology in Dutch Speaking Countries

Edited by

J. Van Houtte

1985 **MARTINUS NIJHOFF PUBLISHERS**
a member of the KLUWER ACADEMIC PUBLISHERS GROUP
DORDRECHT / BOSTON / LANCASTER

Distributors

for the United States and Canada: Kluwer Academic Publishers, 190 Old Derby Street, Hingham, MA 02043, USA
for the UK and Ireland: Kluwer Academic Publishers, MTP Press Limited, Falcon House, Queen Square, Lancaster LA1 1RN, UK
for all other countries: Kluwer Academic Publishers Group, Distribution Center, P.O. Box 322, 3300 AH Dordrecht, The Netherlands

Library of Congress Cataloging in Publication Data

Main entry under title:

Sociology of law and legal anthropology in the
   Dutch speaking countries.

   (Nijhoff law specials)
   Bibliography: p.
   1. Sociological jurisprudence--Addresses, essays,
lectures. 2. Ethnological jurisprudence--Addresses,
essays, lectures. 3. Law--Netherlands--Addresses,
essays, lectures. I. Houtte, J. van, 1934-   .
II. Series.
K376.S655 1985   340'.115   85-8878
ISBN 90-247-3175-5

ISBN 90-247-3175-5 (this volume)

Copyright

PRINTED IN THE NETHERLANDS

Contents

List of Contributors

Editor:
J. Van Houtte
Professor, University of Antwerp (UFSIA-UIA)

Authors:
R. Abel
Professor, School of Law, University of California, Los Angeles

E. Blankenburg
Professor, University of Amsterdam

C. Cozijn, W.O.D.C.,
Ministry of Justice, The Hague

J. Griffiths
Professor, University of Groningen

M. Gysels
Assistant, University of Antwerp (UFSIA)

Preface

J. Van Houtte, editor

The annual meeting of the Research Committee on Sociology of Law of the International Sociological Association took place in Antwerp from September 7 to 10, 1983.

The aim of the meeting was to make the sociology of law research activities in the Dutch-speaking countries more widely known – a goal to which the present publication is intended to contribute. Indeed, the work done in the field of the sociology of law in Dutch by scholars in the Netherlands, and the Flemish parts of Belgium is far less known outside those countries than its quantity, scope and quality deserve.

In a general introduction E. Blankenburg sketches the general situation of the sociology of law research in the 1980s compared to that of the glorious 1970s.

R. Abel, an American sociologist, was asked, as a privileged observer, to sketch the sociology of law activities in the Dutch-speaking countries. Abel's nationality affords him a measure of distance, but he has, over the years, always entertained frequent contacts with the Dutch-speaking sociologists.

The first part reports on the sociology of law in the Low Countries. A trend report was dedicated, respectively, to procedural law (E. Blankenburg) and the institutes of family law (J. Van Houtte/C. Cozijn). A bibliography of publications since 1970 was composed by M. Gysels. The Dutch-language titles were translated into English.

The second part deals with legal anthropology. The trend report and related bibliography are by J. Griffiths.

The present publication has been made possible thanks to the efforts of many. Financial aid was extended by the Belgian National Fund for Scientific Research and the Belgian Ministry of Education. Mrs. L. Meynckens took care of the administrative tasks.

Sociology of Law in the 1980s compared to the glorious 1970s

Address to the meeting of the
Research Committee on Sociology of Law in Antwerp, September 1982

E. BLANKENBURG

Today we have been listening to an impressive array of research reports. They give evidence of very creative years which lie behind us. Evaluating them, We have to admit to many faults and criticisms. But, on the whole, we may say that in the member-countries represented here, sociologists of law have deserved their reputation as being an especially active and unsettling crew of research oriented people among legal scholars.

If we look into the future, we cannot promise that such a level of activity can be maintained as we have in the 70s. The reason for my giving this evaluation in place of our colleague, Glastra van Loon from Den Haag might serve as an indicator of the increasing tensions in all of our universities these day. Glastra van Loon is presenting – this very afternoon – an interdisciplinary research project before the Dutch national research fund. He has to defend it against competing demands from other faculties, all of which have reasonable research proposals. I can still remember times in the 1970s when funding for research was more abundant than researchers able to do good work. These days, this seems incredible. In the last years, we have experienced a simultaneous increase of demand and decrease of supply of research funds, simply because universities are looking for a way to pay the people they have been forced to let go. At a time when more and more research demands are arriving at the funding institutions, we are experiencing serious cuts in almost every source of funding which many of us depended on in the 70s.

I am not going to bore you with general statements about the general resession in the universities. My remarks concern the specific resession that sociology of law is going through. After listening to our discussions today and to the panels on Flemish and Dutch contributions to sociology of law, one might get the impression that with so much activity and research going on, the situation in sociology of law cannot be that bad. Indeed, the research summaries presented today indicate a considerable achievement. But it is an achievement based on research started and financed during the 1970s. If we project ourselves into the future and ask how much research we shall be able to report in 1987 (in other words, research that has to get underway now) I am afraid that we shall have to expect much less.

Hopefully, however, we shall not have to say the same of the level of quality of our research. Economic resession always means that there will be less research. But is does not necessarily mean that research output must be qualitatively worse. Lack of resources can, on the contrary;, even be a stimulus to do better work. (Not only in the sense of doing "good work", but also in the methodological sense. We might not do as much data gathering, but might concentrate instead on more careful interpretation and more theorizing about our data. In the 1970s, we very often had more expensive data gathering than time to carefully evaluate them. Now we might concentrate on doing more careful theoretical work on data we already have.)

A change of methodology will also mean a change of emphasis on which topics are to be studied. Some of the papers discussed today (like those on anthropology of law or those on language analysis in court proceedings) indicate the emphasis which researchers in our field might turn to in the coming years. There are less expensive, more single-researcher projects, but they seem very promising nevertheless.

Turning away from large quantity research to small, quality methodology is a consequence of the difficulties sociologists of law encounter in all of our countries in continuing work in the 1980s. We are a small field, not well institutionalized, with few institutes or university chairs in any of our member-countries (with the exception maybe of Italy, next to which I would name the Netherlands as the country where our field is *relatively* well established). In most countries, we sociologists of law have largely been living off the wealth of the growing social science disciplines of the 1970s. Today social scientists, especially sociologists, are under heavy pressure to reduce their activities and dismiss their collaborators. (In the Netherlands, entire faculties of sociology and applied sociology are being dissolved.)

Competition for research funds for sociologists has become a competition for survival. Sociology of law finds itself in a relatively lucky position as many of us are connected to law schools, not to sociology departments. If we look at the number of students choosing their field of study, the recent years have experienced a trend of sharply reduced numbers of students in sociology, but at least at this time increasing numbers of students in law. As students become increasingly job oriented, they might consider sociology of law marginal in comparison to courses on civil, notary, or tax law. Thus, *within* the law schools with respect to teaching as well as to legal sciences we might as sociologists of law be somewhat marginal, but *with* the law school, we are in a relatively safe position with a wide field of topics for teaching at an enormous array of research questions to be followed up.

The itinerary of our meeting today has given an impression of how diverse the topics in our field are. They derive from the numerous offers of cooperation with colleagues in their respective specific areas of law, with advocates and judges asking research advice on problems arising from the development of their professions and with legislators trying to predict the effects of their professions and with legislators trying to predict the effects of their lawmaking. To give an example of this from the session which I have been chairing this morning on the field of "theories of litigation": here, we are presented with some growth as consequence of the public fiscal crises. In all of our countries, there are complaints about increasing caseloads in the courts, some of the increase being related to economic tensions, but not all of them by any means. The societal reasons leading to more litigation should be one of the topics of sociologists of law looking into such factors as increasing labour mobility, of increasing divorce rates, of rising state interference, and consequently increasing complaints and procedures against the decisions of government agencies. In my opinion, many of the factors leading to increasing workloads of courts are induced externally, they are inherent in societal developments and shall not vanish with the end of economic resession. Thus, while many sectors of economy are shrinking, even while government spending might be shrinking, the judiciary will remain a growing industry and law schools will continue to draw students. We sociologists of law will have to give an explanation for this trend of legal institution counter to much of the deregulation and de-governmentalisation rhetoric of our days. Sociological studies of litigation should also be able to contribute to solving some of the procedural and organisational problems arising from the massive increase of court procedures with the resulting increase of routine, of pre-fabricated decisions in more and more automatised areas of justice and of the changes this brings about the work of judges and of advocates and for their concept of what law is.

But I do not want to close with purely pragmatic questions. Our discussion on legal procedures has continuously stressed that legal problems are defined quite differently according to the social context out of which they arise and according to the infra-structure of institutions which determine what is the distinctively legal about them. Continuously we have been trying to place legal conflict handling in the context of other – for lack of a better word they are called "social" – conflict institutions. The session on anthropology of law which took place this afternoon focused on such contexts and the different meanings which the concept of "legal procedure" take in different societies. Let me therefore end with a reminder: as sociologists we shall place any theory of legal procedure and theory of legal institutions into the context of more general patterns of social organisation. We shall stress that legal procedures and legal reasoning are special cases of discourse and of decision. If we want to communicate with our colleague in legal sciences, we have to stand both inside and outside of their discourse. We have to discuss with them which of our insights make a difference within the frame of legal reasoning. The so-called "sociological jurisprudence" is such a discourse within jurisprudence which refers to the contributions not only of sociologists of law but of social scientists in general.

Sociologists of law have an additional task in the communication with our colleagues in the law schools: we look at the legal profession and their organisation of discourse also from the outside. We are not only engaged in a discourse *within* legal science, but also *on* the legal sciences. That is not always comfortable for those which we make an object of our studies, even though it seems to me necessary for any discipline (including our own) to have somebody to evaluate it from the outside, and thus help to engage in self-rejection. Considering the relatively fortunate position which sociologists of law have at the margins of law schools and legal sciences, I want to conclude with my thanks for the interest and sometimes patience with which our colleagues in the legal profession keep listening to us.

Sociology of law in the Dutch-speaking countries

R. ABEL

The sociology of law written in Dutch by scholars in the Netherlands, the Flemish parts of Belgium, and Indonesia is far less well known outside those countries than it deserves to be by reason of its quantity, scope, and quality. In order to overcome the barriers of ignorance, distance, and language, the recent meeting of the ISA Research Committee on Sociology of Law in Antwerp (September 7-10, 1983) presented a broad overview of research by Dutch-speaking scholars – recently completed, in progress, and proposed. I will draw on the two reports distributed at that meeting (Centre, 1983; NNR, 1983) in order to summarize the topics addressed and the findings presented and try to place them in the context of work in English. The research conveniently can be grouped under five broad headings, even though particular projects often span two or more: knowledge and opinion about law, law in action, legal aid, courts and litigation, and anthropology of law.

Knowledge and opinion about law

This was one of the first topics investigated by Dutch-speaking sociologists of law, as part of an early collaborative cross-cultural effort by European scholars – the so-called KOL studies (Podgorecki et al., 1973). Although the issue remains theoretically interesting (cf. Sarat, 1977), most contemporary inquiry tends to be merely an instrumental aspect of an applied research project examining the efficacy and acceptance of an existing rule or the extent of popular support by a contemplated rule change. Thus the Research and Documentation Center of the Dutch Ministry of Justice has studied public opinion about what financial provision ought to be made for a widow after the death of her husband and discovered that a broad consensus favors strengthening her control over the estate, at least during her lifetime (Cozijn, 1983: 300-01). Yet this project also revealed that KOL studies offer a very incomplete picture of reality, for favorable but inchoate opinions are not political action, and nothing has been done in this instance to conform existing law to public opinion. The Center also has examined attitudes toward alimony payments to a divorced wife and found, to its surprise, not only that there are few differences between men and women but also that the attitudes of the young are more conservative than those of the old (Id. 302-03). This suggests the need to revise the widely held belief, often attributed to Dicey (1905; cf. Abel, 1982), that law invariably lags behind changes in public opinion. Rather, it seems, public opinion is far from monolithic; the fraction of the public (whether a majority or a minority) whose views are embodied in law secures both normative support and also, perhaps more importantly, a victory in the endless competition among status groups (Gusfield, 1963; Edelman, 1964). Even when the law leads public opinion, the latter acts as a substantial brake and social change: although Dutch women now are entitled to keep their maiden names after marriage, very few do so (younger, better educated professionals), and even they experience considerabvle difficulties (Cozijn, 1983: 304-05). It is clear that considerable dissonance between law and opinion can persist indefinitely. A Belgian study found, not surprisingly, that a majority of people felt no obligation to report income if not compelled to do so and passed no judgment on those who evaded their legal obligations (Centre, 1983: 3-4; cf. Mason and Calvin, 1978).

Each of these findings was obtained at the behest of policymakers concerned with the efficacy or acceptability of existing laws or the degrees of public support that could be mobilized for reform. But I believe their theoretical contribution lies elsewhere – they constitute data for the creation of a more pluralistic model of law in society, of the kind that legal anthropology has been advocating for years. Norms, institionalized patterns of behavior, and sanctions derive from many societal levels and structures, of which the state is only one. There undoubtedly are realms of behavior in which state law is almost as dominant as legal positivism proclaims, though many of the examples are fairly trivial – traffic laws, for instance. People drive on the right side of the road because the state orders them to do so and will punish disobedience (if they also act out of an instinct of self-preservation); the state unilaterally can change the rule from left-hand to right-hand driving and secure 100 percent compliance – as occurred in Sweden. And the feeling that it is "proper" to drive on one side of the road or the other is entirely an artifact of positive law. But in most areas of social life, especially those about which people care most deeply, several different structures simultaneously generate overlapping and often inconsistent norms, behaviors, and sanctions. Family law obviously is subordinate to kinship structures. Even the sense of an obligation to contribute to the public treasury derives less from positive law and more from community mores and the taxpayer's particular economic role and position. Thus KOL studies urge us to redefine law so as to direct attention to the social fields (of which the state is only one) within which a given behavior receives its normative significance and social reinforcement.

Law in action

KOL studies explore one dimension of what Eugen Ehrlich called the living law and what contemporary sociologists and lawyers refer to as law in action, to distinguish it from the law in books. Law in action is the constellation of state rules, the state institutions that declare and enforce those rules, and, most importantly, the sphere of social action the rules purport to address. Here, again, the impetus for research tends to be practical rather than theoretical, concerned less with legal institutions themselves than with the behaviors they address. As is true in the English-speaking traditions (Abel, 1980: 816), scholarly interest tends to be preoccupied with criminal behavior (Cozijn, 1983: 299) and with family relationships. It is not clear whether this focus expresses a judgment that the most pressing social problems are to be found in those areas or whether concern with those areas actually serves to divert attention from other more intractable social tensions – or the most likely explanation – whether social scientists simply find those areas easier to understand and more accessible to social investigation. But it seems strange to devote most of our energies to studying the impact of law on modes of behavior (such as relations between intimates) that we would expect, intuitively, to be relatively impervious to such remote influence and to neglect, by comparison, behavior that is more susceptible to influence through a calculus of positive and negative sanctions, such as economic activity.

In Belgium, studies of law in action have combined these two spheres by looking at the nature of economic relations among kin. Thus the Center for Sociology of Law in Antwerp has examined the financial support of the elderly (Centre, 1983: 5-7; Van Houtte and Breda, 1978). It traced the transformation of this legal obligation from preservation of the social status of the particular elderly ascendant (a nineteenth century residue of Roman law traditions) into a national uniform minimum level of support. But notwithstanding this change in the expected direction – from particularistic to universalistic – the law still maintains the fiction that the obligation is owed by the particular descendants rather than by society as a whole. Yet few of the elderly seek to enforce this obligation; state institutions become involved only when the family relationship is strained by other causes; and even then, descendants contribute only a fraction of the total maintenance. Virtually everyone involved – social workers, lawyers, and the family members themselves – believe that the financial obligation should be borne by the impersonal welfare apparatus rather than the particular family unit. A similar set of conclusions is prompted by a Belgian study of the financial relationships among divorced spouses. (Centre, 1983: 7-9; Van Houtte and De Vocht, 1981-82; cf. Cozijn, 1983: 301-03). Here, again, once the social bond has been undermined by physical and legal separation (as the bond between generations is weakened by physical distance, cultural change, and individualism), the economic obligation also becomes attenuated: payments of spousal and child support are inadequate in amount and irregular (cf. Chambers, 1977, 1979; Lempert, 1981-82). A further parallel between the two is the marked social ambivalence about whether the support obligation ought to be particularistic or universalistic. A majority of the public feel strongly that the former husband's financial responsibility should depend on whether he was "at fault" in the marital dissolution. (Those who have experienced divorce first-hand disagree; as the divorce rate rises, therefore, the emphasis on fault should diminish.) On the other hand, a minority want a time limit on any spousal obligation, and most feel that the wife is entitled only to a minimum level of maintenance, not to the standard of living she enjoyed while married. Thus we can expect that this financial obligation, too, increasingly will be shouldered by the state.

The difficulty of using law instrumentally to change family behavior is well illustrated by the 1969 amendment to the Belgian law of adoption (Centre, 1983: 9-11; Van Houtte, 1983). The declared purpose of that reform was to encourage adoptions, particularly of hard-to-place children. A superficial view might suggest it was successful, for the number of adoptions increased dramatically. But most of these were regularizations of existing relationships: natural mothers adopting children conceived out of wedlock or step-fathers adopting the children of a wife who had been married previously. (Both of those behaviors had extra-legal causes: increases in the frequency of sexual relations and cohabitation before marriage and in the divorce rate.) Only a third of all adoptions were heterofamilial, and, for several reasons, the numbers have been declining, both absolutely and relative to the regularization of pre-existing relationships. One constraint is supply: contraception and abortion have greatly reduced the number of children available. Another is the reluctance of judges to terminate the rights of birth parents against their wishes, even when the child has been out of their custody for a long time. A third problem is the reluctance of institutions to deplete the number of children in care, which would threaten the raison d'être of those institutions (cf. Pocar and Ronfani, 1978: 612-18). But demand also exerts constraints: childless adoptive parents insist on adopting children who resemble them as closely as possible; it is only parents with their own birth children who are interested in the growing pool of potential adoptees from immigrant families; and few parents of either kind are willing to adopt the physically or socially handicapped children who were a prime concern of the law. Thus personal and social norms remain far more influential than official rules.

If law is ineffective in shaping the creation of family relationships, it is even more peripheral when the relationships are ongoing, even if in attenuated form. Thus the Center for Sociology of Law in Antwerp writes "The 14th of July 1976 had to be a great day for Belgian women" (Centre, 1983: 12; Gijsels and Vogels, 1982) because the legislature enacted a law abrogating the residue of juridical inequality between spouses. But for all the considerable symbolic significance of such legislation (witness the emotional furor surrounding the ultimately unsuccessful campaign to pass the Equal Rights Amendment to the U.S. Constitution), it appears that relations between spouses depend far more on extra-legal factors. Wives have gained whatever financial independence they enjoy largely by entering the workforce. Although decisions concerning the disposition of family income and the management of property are made jointly and with equal participation, the execution of decisions tends generally to display more traditional sex stereotypes. Decision-making and execution is likely to be more equal to the extent that the spouses are recently married, the wife has a relatively high level of education, a modern attitude, and an occupation, and the husband has a relatively high status occupation. The marginality of law is pronounced even when the legal relationship between the spouses formally has been dissolved. A Dutch study found that couples seek a judicial order concerning child visitation by the non-custodial parent in only 15 percent of divorces involving children, and that half of those orders merely confirm a parental agreement (Griffiths, 1983a: 362). Regardless of whether an order has been entered, the divorced parents strongly prefer to organize visitation arrangements themselves, without the intervention of the court or even of their lawyers (who are used mainly for property matters); such extra-legal arrangements have a much better change of elicting compliance and satisfaction than do judicial orders (Id. 368).

The one study of this genre that does not concern family law confirms the insight that the legal arena overlaps and is in tension with other social fields. This Dutch investigation of immigration law (van Groenendahl, 1983) has the virtue of exploring both the relatively neglected subject of legislation (cf. Abel, 1980: 816) and the more familiar topic of its admiration. With the recession of the early 1970s, the Netherlands, like other industrialized northern European countries, had to decide what to do about the large number of migrant workers, both legal and illegal immigrants, who no longer were needed by the economy. This decision was enormously revealing about the political, and moral issues, as well as tension between the strategic desirability of secrecy and fidelity to democratic ideals. But the other lesson of this story may be even more important: that politics does not end with the passage of legislation. The administration of the new law was subject to continuing pressures: first the successful demand for special treatment by the so-called Church Moroccans; then the demand by other immigrants for like treatment; the need to delegate decision-making to street-level bureaucrats because of the enormous caseload; the inability of the central government to supervise the exercise of individual discretion; and the capacity of lawyers to challenge such unconstrained discretion by reference to legalistic procedural rules. The unhappy experience of Dutch officials –

who called it "a black page in the history of the *Ministry of Justice*" (van Groenendael, 1983: 353) – suggests another generalization: a law that lacks a principled foundation (no persuasive reasons were offered for the distinctions between immigrants who were offered legal residence and those who were not) cannot be administered in a principled fashion (no plausible answer can be given to those excluded who now demand special treatment).

Legal aid

Studies of knowledge and opinion about law and the law in action tend to be dominated by interest in other social problems; law is merely an instrumental mechanism (whose utility probably is exaggerated). One of the first legal institutions to attract the attention of social scientists – legal aid – also was inspired by an extrinsic concern with broadening and equalizing access to law (Schuyt et al., 1976, 1977; Griffiths, 1977). The substantial investment of scholarly energies in studying the Dutch legal aid system may reflect the fact that it was the earliest scheme on the Continent (established in 1957, eight years after the British program) and still represents the largest per capita expenditure. The system has grown significantly in several different directions during the last decade and a half. The first innovation, which arguably stimulated the others, was the law shops founded by law students in the 1970s (Bruinsma, 1983; see also Garth, 1980: 118-24; Cooper, 1983: 45-55). These were offices staffed by volunteers in the evenings and on the weekends, offering free advice to both individuals and groups. In the peak year of 1974, they claim to have counseled 60,000 clients (Bruinsma, 1983: 333). But, like so many "alternative" institutions, they have suffered one of two fates: routinization or a dwindling commitment and disappearance. Bruinsma argues that the second innovation, the BvR (Buro voor Rechtshulp – Legal Aid Office) – a front line service providing free advice and referrals to private lawyers under the judicare plan – was introduced by the government in order to displace the more radical and autonomous law shops, and he quotes the highest civil servant in the Ministry of Justice as declaring: "We regularized the social unrest and the law shop movement into public legal services, which became part of the existing legal system." (Id. 332). The budget of the BvR grew from half a million guilders in 1975 to 23 million in 1982, and today there are 42 Buro with more than 187 advisers (van de Beek et al., 1983: 310, 312). The BvR are dominated by the Ministry of Justice (which exerts pressure for uniformity) and the legal profession (which obtains a significant amount of judicare business through referrals from the Buro); the association of Buro staff (Vereniging voor Rechtshulp – which interestingly excludes nonlawyers) is relatively weak. In order to evaluate the impact of the BvR, one study compared their clientele with that of the Citizens Advice Bureaux (Instituten Sociaal Raadslieden), which expanded enormously during the 1970s in order to guide beneficiaries of the rapidly growing Dutch welfare state through the maze of rules and bureaucracy (Id. 307, 309). The two institutions handle about 250,000 cases a year each (Id. 307; Bruinsma, 1983: 333). But though the BvR have made a determined effort to reach the more deprived segments of the population (Bruinsma, 1983: 336), in practice their clientele has a higher proportion of men than that of the Citizens Advice Bureaux; they are younger, more likely to be employed, and better educated (van de Beek et al., 1983: 308). Furthermore, the matters that clients bring to the BvR are more legal and complex, the claims are more salient, and the client is more likely to be proactice rather than reactive. One reason for the difference appears to be ease of access: the 37 Citizens Advice Bureaux are geographically more dispersed (Id. 309, 322-23). Although the BvR has tended to displace both the law shops and the trade unions as a provider of legal advice (Blankenburg, 1983: 245), unlike those institutions, it does little or no group representation (Bruinsma, 1983: 336). Furthermore, the quality of individual advice is poor (Id. 337-38). Finally, like all facets of the welfare state, legal aid is at the mercy of political and economic forces: its growth has been halted and cuts have been made as a result of the current recession and the political turn to the right (Id. 340). Interestingly, whereas in the United States similar pressures have diverted resources from staffed offices to judicare on the (fictitious) ground of cost efficiency, in the Netherlands there is some thought of channeling funds in the opposite direction because the budget of the BvR can be controlled, but the judicare program is a blank check on which any eligible client can draw. These cuts also have been justified by the argument that legal aid fuels the "litigation crisis," even though Dutch civil litigation and criminal prosecution rates remain the lowest in Europe (Blankenburg, 1983: 241).

The contrast between legal aid in Belgium and the Netherlands could not be more extreme. Although both are welfare states and possess similar economies, the Netherlands has the most extensive system of state supported legal aid on the Continent while Belgium has *none*, although free services are provided through non-state institutions. A tradition of pro deo services (a statutory obligation) still is observed, though these are provided mainly in family matters by recently qualified lawyers and tend to be quite cursory (Centre, 1983: 16-17; Breda, 1983). The Belgium law shop movement has paralleled the rise and decline of its larger counterpart in the Netherlands. On the other hand, many other social institutions provide legal services: unions, elected officials, the consumer movement, and (unique to Belgium) social assistance agencies. With the exception of the last, these agencies tend to overlook the most deprived sectors of the community. Jef Breda has offered two plausible explanations for the absence of state intervention in the delivery of legal services. First, the fact that there are twice as many lawyers per population in Belgium as in the Netherlands renders the services of the former considerably cheaper and thus more accessible through the private market. Second, Belgium has a tradition of delivering most social services (e.g., health, education, housing, even welfare benefits) through private organizations out of respect for the major linguistic, religious, and cultural divisions in Belgian society.

If these studies have been preoccupied with who obtains what kind of legal services, some attention has been paid to the impact of legal aid on the profession – an impact that obviously affects the characteristics of the far larger proportion of legal services that is delivered through the private market. The significance of judicare for the Dutch profession cannot be exaggerated. Total expenditures grew from 45.4 million guilders in 1975 to 178.7 in 1982 (van de Beek, 1983: 312), or an average of more than 4,000 guilderss per lawyer. But in fact, the work is very unevenly distributed: about 10 percent of the profession obtain all their income from judicare, and many other practices earn half their income from that source (Bruinsma, 1983: 338). Nevertheless, the 90 percent of the profession that obtains most of its income from the private market has been scanted by social scientists and deserves to be made the object of future research (but see Klijn, 1981; Blankenburg, 1983: 245).

Courts and litigation

Courts are a natural focus of socio-legal interest, for their functions are at the core of the legitimacy of the local system. The ideology of liberal legalism contains a number of criteria that judicial processes must satisfy. Perhaps the most important is the notion that decisions reflect the dictates of laws, not the preferences of men. Because this ideal runs counter to the insights of the legal realists about the maleability and indeterminacy of legal concepts and fact-finding, Dutch studies have explored the influence of judicial backgrounds on decisions and discerned only a weak relationship (Blankenburg, 1983: 258). A subsequent investigation examined the ways in which experimental subjects select information in deciding hypothetical cases and found significant variation in the amount of information requested but were unable to correlate this with differences in personal characteristics (van Koppen and ten Kate, 1983: 274-75, 278). Other inequities can distort the judicial process – geographic variation for instance – and the response has been efforts to ensure prosecutorial uniformity throughout the Netherlands (Blankenburg, 1983: 252-54). But even if rules are uniform and judges adhere to them faithfully, bias still may emerge: variables that predict recidivism for purposes of criminal sentencing may single out the working class for harsher punishments (Id. 253). A second criterion of justice is that the decision-making process should be comprehensible to the parties. By this standard Dutch justice fares no better than that of other countries: parties have great difficulty understanding the judicial process, and their comprehension undermines its legitimacy (Id. 248, 251-52).

An alternative mode of legitimation (which subordinates and indeed contradicts the ideal of legalism) is to stress the democratic or populist nature of decison-making. This has been particularly pronounced in areas where an individual claimant is at an obvious and pronounced disadvantage, for instance, when confronting an employer or the state (Centre, 1983: 15; Roos, 1983a; 1983b). Thus the Netherlands introduced lay judges in employer-employee conflicts in order to pacify both interest groups (Roos, 1983b: 394). In practice they have little influence on either process or outcome, although they may be more sympathetic to litigants than are professional judges; their primary function appears to be to enhance the image of the organizations that appoint them (Id. 395-402). On the other hand, although law adjudication appears inconsistent with the formal rationality that Weber argued was essential to capitalism, this may suggest a problem with the theory rather than the data. Large organizations do require certainty and predictability, but they secure these conditions outside of court and in the routine processing that characterizes the vast bulk of most trial court dockets (Roos, 1983a: 3856-87). Even when lay judges have a formal role to play, they do not hear these uncontroversial cases, and, in the more difficult matters, they defer to professionals (Roos, 1983b: 395-402).

If studies of court naturally begin with judges, the next step is to recognize that others actors may play significant roles. The courtroom regulars inevitably develop a social structure and subculture that influences the behavior of each (Blankenburg, 1983: 251-52). But it is the litigants themselves who have come to take center stage. One reason for the interest in litigant behavior is the fact they determine litigation rates, and concern over rising rates is pervasive today (Galanter, 1983). A Belgian study of civil litigation found that lawyers and civil litigation both have been growing faster than the population whereas judges have been growing more slowly – a combination that might well produce problems (except for the fact that litigation grew more rapidly in the nineteenth century, when no one apparently thought this signified a crisis, than it has in the twentieth) (Centre, 1983: 14). Increasing rates of litigation and prosecution are troubling because in Continental legal systems, unlike those of the United States and perhaps England, there is a much lower rate of attrition of cases after they are filed (Blankenburg, 1983: 250). One response to the so-called litigation explosion has been to create alternatives to the court; but the uniform experience has been that these increase overall caseload rather than diverting cases from the court (Id. 249). And commentators have noted that the increase in litigation may express an increase in social conflict rather than some defect in the legal system (Id. 261).

The principal interest in litigants, however, has been whether their confrontations assume recognizable patterns and whether these correlate with outcomes. The central hypothesis, of course, has been that of Marc Galanter (1974). Attempts have been made to operationalize the concepts of individual and organized parties and one-shot and repeatplayers. These have confirmed that the most frequent dyad is an organized repeatplayer claiming against an individual one-shot defendant and that the success rate of the former is very high (Jettinghof, 1983). On the other hand, when the individual one-shot claimant seeks redress against the organized repeatplayer, the likelihood of success is low (Id.: Centre, 1983: 15). In both situations, the process is highly routinized, and many claims are won or lost by the default of the other party (Jettinghof, 1983: 287, 292). Yet a core of contested cases remains that is not handled routinely; these typically pit one organized party against another and tend to be found in the higher or appellate courts (Ibid; cf. Macaulay, 1977). Exceptions to this model – organized commercial actors who abstain from using the courts although their business lends itself to routinized claims – suggest that further refinements of this powerful generalization are required.

Anthropology of law

It is not possible to summarize John Griffith's (1983b) 100-page survey of the history, institutional structure, personnel, findings, and future prospects of anthropology of law in the Netherlands, but perhaps I can indicate some of his principal arguments. Anthropology of law had its roots in the colonial experience and the need of administrators for accurate information about the norms and institutions of the people they were governing. With the end of colonialism, no justification remains for the separation between anthropological and sociological studies of law. Indeed, Griffiths makes an eloquent and persuasive argument that each would be enriched by borrowing the methods and outlook of the other. The strengths of the anthropological tradition are manifold: it focused on the microprocesses of social interaction, which it described in rich detail; it stressed the inescapably pluralistic nature of all legal systems; and it insisted that an adequate understanding of law must be both comparative and historical. In all these respects it is a necessary complement to a sociological tradition that: often deals in aggregates and quantified variables, which necessarily lose much of the richness and complexity of social life; is unjustifiably blinkered in its preoccupation with state law; and is culturally parochial and ahistorical. The comparative perspective of anthropology constantly reminds us of the need to look beyond the folk concepts of the system with which we are familiar in order to develop analytic concepts that are not tainted with local idiosyncracies. On the other hand, the strength of sociology is its connection with pressing contemporary social problems which, for metropolitan scholars, are situated at home rather than abroad. The insights of anthropology are particularly appropriate to the problems of western pluralistic societies, such as the treatment of immigrant groups by the national legal system and the functioning of non-state legal systems within those communities themselves.

Conclusion

The Dutch-speaking tradition in sociology of law has great strengths and deserves wider recognition by the international community. It is quite possible that the concentration of Dutch-speaking socio-legal scholars is greater, in proportion to the population they are studying, than that in any other country. The research produced thus far has been impressive in both quantity and quality. It displays thorough familiarity with the writing in English and German in a way that neither of those literatures adequately reciprocates. The limitations under which Dutch researchers labor are familiar to scholars everywhere – insufficient funding and governmental insistence that research must be directed to narrowly pragmatic questions before it will be supported. In the present economic and political situation, these obstacles are not likely to diminish. Yet I think that much can be done with the interesting data already gathered and that questions of broader theoretical significance fruitfully can be pursued through the synthesis and reanalysis of the wealth of information in Dutch on the operation of law in Belgium, the Netherlands, and the former Dutch colonies.

References

Abel, R.L. (1980). "Redirecting Social Studies of Laws." 14 Law & Society Review 805.
Abel, R.L. (1982). "Law as Lag: Inertia as a Social Theory of Law." 80 Michigan Law Review 785.
Blankenburg, E. (1983). "The Role of Sociology of Law in Reforming Procedural Law: An Annoted Bibliography." 4 NNR 241.
Breda, J. (1983). "Legal Aid in Belgium." 4 NNR 360.
Centre of Sociology of Law 1983 10 Years Survey of Research. Antwerp: University of Antwerp-UFSIA.
Chambers, D. (1977). "Men Who Know They are Watched: Some Benefits and Costs of Jailing for Nonpayment of Support." 75 Michigan Law Review 900.

18

Chambers, D. (1979). Making Fathers Pay: The Enforcement of Child Support. Chicago: University of Chicago Press.

Cooper, J. (1983). Public Legal Services: A Comparative Study of Policy, Politics, and Practice. London: Sweet & Maxwell.

Cozijn, C. (1983). "Research in the Sociology of Law at the Research and Documentation Centre of the Ministry of Justice in the Netherlands." 4 NNR 299.

Dicey, A.V. (1905). Law and Public Opinion in England During the Nineteenth Century. London: Macmillan.

Edelman, M. (1964). The Symbolic Uses of Politics. Urbana, Il.: University of Illinois Press.

Galanter, M. (1974). "Why the 'Haves' Come Out Ahead: Speculations on the Limits of Legal Change." 9 Law & Society Review 95.

Galanter, M. (1983). "Reading the Landscape of Disputes: What We Know and Don't Know (But Think We Know) about our Allegedly Contentions and Litigious Society." 31 UCLA Law Review 4.

Garth, B. (1980). Neighborhood Legal Services for the Poor. Alphen aan den Rijn: Sijthoff and Noordhoff.

Griffiths, J. (1977). "The Distribution of Legal Services in the Netherlands." 4 British Journal of Law and Society 260.

Griffiths, J. (1983a). "Research in Progress: The Processes by which Divorcing Parents Arrange the Future of their Children, in particular Visitation." 4 NNR 362.

Griffiths, J. (1983b). "Anthropology of Law in the Netherlands in the 1970s." 4 NNR 132.

Gusfield, J. (1963). Symbolic Crusade: Status Politics and the American Temperance Movement. Urbana, Il.: University of Illinois Press.

Gijsels, M., M. Vogels (1982). "Belgian husbands and wives: Equal in patrimonial matters?," 10 International Journal of Sociology of law, 205-216.

Jettinghof, A. (1983). "Clients of the Courts: Some data on parties in civil litigation in the Netherlands." 4 NNR 283.

Klijn, A. (1981). De Balie geschetst: Verslag van een door het WODC gehouden schriftelijke enquête onder de Nederlandse advocatuur (Portrait of the Bar: Report of a Survey of Dutch Advocates). The Hague: WODC.

Lempert, R. (1981-82). "Organizing for Deterrence: Lessons from a Study of Child Support." 16 Law & Society Review 513.

Macaulay, S. (1977). "Elegant Models, Empirical Pictures, and the Complexities of Contract." 11 Law & Society Review 507.

Mason, R.B., L.D. Calvin (1978). "A Study of Admitted Income Tax Evasion." 13 Law & Society Review 73.

NNR (1983). Nieuwsbrief voor Nederlandstalige Rechtssociologen, Rechtsantropologen en Rechtspsychologen, volume 4, number 2.

Pocar, V., P. Ronfani (1978). "Family Law in Italy: Legislative Innovation and Social Change." 12 Law & Society Review 607.

Podgorecki, A., N. Kaupen, J. Van Houtte, P. Vinke and B. Kutchinsky (1973). Knowledge and Opinion about Law. Oxford: Martin Robertson.

Roos, N.N.M. (1983a). "Weber's Views Concerning Lay Adjudication Considered in the Light of Empirical Research." 4 NNR 376.

Roos, N.N.M. (1983b). "Summary of Lekenrechters (Lay Judges): Een empirisch onderzoek naar hert functioneren van de lekenrechters bij de raden van beroep voor de Sociale Verzekeringen (An empirical study of the functioning of law judges in the social insurance tribunals)." 4 NNR 392.

Sarat, A. (1977). "Studying American Legal Culture." 11 Law & Society Review 427.

Schuyt, K., K. Groenendijk, B. Sloot (1976). De Weg Naar Het Recht. Deventer: Kluwer.

Schuyt, K. (1977). "Access to the Legal System and Legal Services Research." 1977 European Yearbook in Law and Sociology 98.

Van de Beek, E.C. G.B.M. Enbersen, R.J. van der Veen (1983). "Participant Observation in Advice Bureaux." 4 NNR 307.

Van Groenendael, T. "Legalizing Illegal Aliens: A Case Study of Regulatory Justice." 4 NNR 347.

Van Houtte, J. (1983). "Inaction of Law: The Belgian Adoption Law." 4 NNR 296.

Van Houtte, J., J. Breda (1978). "Financial Support of the Aged by their Adult Children: The Family as a Residual Agency in the Solution of Poverty in Belgium." 12 Law & Society Review 645.

Van Houtte, J. (1981-82). "The Obligation to Provide Maintenance between Divorced Husband and Wife in Belgium." 16 Law & Society Review 321.

Van Koppen, P.J., J. ten Kate (19893). "Use of Informationl by the Private Law Judge: an attributional model of judicial decision-making." 4 NNR 262.

PART ONE

Sociology of law

The role of sociology of law in reforming procedural law in the Law Countries: Trend report

E. BLANKENBURG

Sociology of law is represented by a chair or at least a lectureship in every law faculty in the Netherlands, in Flemish Belgium by two sizable research centres in Antwerpen and Leuven. Important research is also done by the Dutch "Research and Documentation Centre" of the Ministry of Justice in Den Haag (WODC). Legal journals pay considerable attention to empirical research, and there is frequent reference to social research in legal argumentation. Considering the small size of the social systems which make up the Dutch-speaking legal communities, considering them being part of two different national legal systems, sociology of law can be viewed as well developed and amazingly well integrated. In absolute size, however, the number of those who research in the socio-legal is small. For this reason, sociologists have not been able to research all the problems that procedural reforms might present. Still, the intake of foreign legal and research development is quick and thorough because of the widespread knowledge of other languages and cultures.

The input of a social science community into legal policy formation has been demonstrated in the 1970s first in the Netherlands, somewhat later also in Belgium in the vehement discussion of reform in matters of access to law. It has led to a legal aid movement within the advocacy which has no equivalent on the rest of the European continent. This intellectual climate also led to serious discussion questioning the formality of legal procedure and the possibilities of avoiding judicial institutions in favour of what is called "diversion" or "alternative" solutions. Again, we have to stress the differences of the Belgian compared to the Dutch situation: legal institutions of Belgium resemble very much the French and German institutions in being elaborate and differentiated, while the Dutch legal tradition has been stressing mediative and informal ways of handling legal conflicts. As indicators for this difference the size of prison population as well as the rate of civil litigation per 100.000 of the population might be mentioned: the Dutch prison population is traditionally very small due to many short prison sentences. Also in civil law matters the Dutch are evidently not very litigation prone. The load of the civil courts (relative to population size) is considerably smaller than that of any other European country. This is even more remarkable as the Netherlands has the most developed system of legal aid on the European continent. Belgium has nothing comparable to offer in terms of public legal aid, but it has developed some legal aid initiated within universities and by local Bar Associations.

However, neither legal aid nor 'alternatives' to court or soft penal policy are solely the merit of sociologists of law. Sociological arguments and empirical research have contributed to their legitimization, but they form only part of the climate of opinion which made the rather careful use of judicial institutions possible. The initiative for the Dutch legal aid schemes came from a broad base within the universities and was fostered in the courts and advocacy by a greater willingness to innovate than could be observed in any other continental legal culture. Therefore, I shall leave it to the reader to choose whether he treats the accepted role of sociology of law as a cause or consequence of a relatively reformist legal policy. It calls for criteria which would enable distinguishing those problems which can satisfactorily be treated as 'legal problems' from those which would more easily be handled by some other forum. Sociology of law evidence also speaks against idealistic hopes that penal procecure could be reformed to the degrees that it resembles communication without social dominance. More realistically, the aim can only be to provide criteria to make legal procedures a little bit more communicative. It would be hopeless to try to achieve equalised communication in a courtroom situation.

Pragmatic questions raised by procedural reforms can lead to basic theories of litigation. I therefore try to relate the questions raised by legal reformists to some of the more basic research on the sociology of litigations done in the Netherlands and in Dutch speaking Belgium in the 1970s.

Access to law in civil and administrative courts

The first study to direct attention to the selectivity of access to the courts was not motivated by procedural law questions, but rather by problems of substantive law of compensation for injury. Bloembergen et al. (1972) chose 1000 cases following traffic accidents from the registers of three court districts in 1967/68. Two-thirds of the cases dealt with damage to cars only; 30% dealt with compensation for injury. More than half of the plaintiffs were insurance companies while 42% were the victim of the accident. The study shows that chance of success for the plaintiffs are very high that about one-third of the procedures end in settlement, every fifth in default, and less than half go all the way to a decision by the court. Even more revealing are the figures on how few accident cases get to court at all. Civil courts were invoked in only 0.4% of all serious traffic accidents (that is with damage of more than 1,000 Dutch Guilders; comparative figures for France are 6,25%, for the Federal Republic of Germany 2%, for the United States 1.5% c.f. p. 12).

Of course such comparisons hinge on how the population of all relevant cases is defined. We could more easily compare accidents with personal injury, and here the share before court is 5% in the Netherlands which again is considerably lower then in any of the countries of comparison. Compensation after traffic accidents is regulated in the Netherlands out of court much more frequently than in countries of comparison. Reasons should be found in the assessment practice of insurance companies and their propensity to take cases before court.

A follow-up study has looked into this: Bloembergen, Van Wersch (1973), reports on 452 interviews with male victims of traffic accidents between 16 and 65 years of age all of whom have suffered personal injury. Most of them have been to a hospital, 13% have paid for treatment themselves, and 5% had to undergo extended rehabilitation treatment. Nevertheless, less than 1% claimed compensation for these costs from whoever caused the accident. Injury was almost exclusively covered by social security and insurance. Beyond those compensation claims were very rare. For example, loss of income was rarely claimed. Only 4% of the workers and their employers suffered major loss of income. Absence from work was largely financed by social security annuity programs and sick-pay from employers. Only 2% claimed any compensation. And, even though one third of all self-employed people suffered income losses, only 20% claimed compensation. One quarter of all damages to cars and motorcycles was covered by the victims' insurance company. Almost half of the damages was paid by the victim himself, though in most cases the amount was small. Discontent with the regulation of claims was mostly directed at the lengthy insurance procedures, hardly ever against their failure to pay or only partly pay for damages. Thus, compensation after traffic accident, is regulated largely without conflicts. Since all of the claims are covered by some form of insurance, few claims remain among those directly involved in the accident. Any claims that a lawyer might think of beyond the normal insurance coverage are not generally perceived by those involved. Compared to legal cultures such as in the US, liability plays a minor role in a welfare state such as the Netherlands. This relieves the courts from much of their potential case-loads.

The research of Bloembergen could have led to more systematical analyses of the conditions of invoking courts. The potential for legal conflicts is always much greater than what is shown in the dockets of the courts. The study demonstrated that conflict-avoiding institutions in the Netherlands are comparatively more expanded than in more litigeous countries. However, the potential of court cases in other than traffic cases remained unknown as well as the reasons why they did not reach courts.

The legal aid movement to document that there is a potential of litigation with low-income people in the 1970s. Critique of middle-class bias of the traditional advocacy was raised by students and young scientists at the Dutch law faculties. It lead in the 1970s to the development of social advocacy which mobilised some of the latent demand for legal aid. The first, very influential document of this critique is to be found in Ars Aequi (X, 1970), a legal journal edited nationwide by law school students. A discussion followed this provocative publication urging the Dutch Ministry of Justice and the Bar to follow a line of careful innovations. The Bar Association supported the development with two reports (Boekman, 1972, 1977).

The Ministry of Justice also helped. It financed Legal Aid Offices; first in Amsterdam, later in all the major cities of the Netherlands, and commissioned research on legal needs from a group of sociologists of law at the university of Nijmegen. The report of Schuyt/Groenendijk/Sloot (1976) forms the most sophisticated study of the international legal needs tradition:

Their book contains a thorough discussion of the various English and American surveys on legal needs and on the frequency of legal contacts. It enumerates four theoretical approaches to explaining the imbalance of upper social classes among lawyer clients:
- the economic barriers of access to lawyers reducing access problems to the inability of paying lawyer and court fees;
- the social-psychological barriers of knowing how to deal with legal institutions;
- the participation barriers, which explains the low number of reported legal problems of the poor, with their overall lower participations in legal activities;
- the participation theory which explains the frequency of legal problems as a function of class bias in which counselling and access institutions (such as lawyers) present themselves to the public.

The analysis of 456 qualitative interviews in three Dutch communities (metropolitan/middle-size town/small town) provides something for each of these theories to explain. It becomes apparent that pure economical barriers explain the least, especially as poverty also leads to sociopsychological barriers, less participation and greater fear of organizational barriers. The new institutions of Dutch Legal Aid in the 1970s therefore include financial subsidy as well as new forms of organization. Subsidy for legal aid to the poor has been paid in moderate volume since 1957 on basis of the law on Legal Aid for People with Minimum Income. In the 1970s the level at which one could qualify for legal aid was raised, so that about 60% of the population was entitled to at least some subsidy for legal aid. Public bureaus for legal aid were instituted in each of the Dutch provinces. The bureaus provide legal information as well as first hand counselling in easy cases. In more complicated cases they have to refer to a local lawyer, who, in turn, may claim fees from the legal aid bureaus under the provision that low income requirements have been fulfilled. This system of referral and subsidy has allowed for a 'social advocacy' to develop in the Netherlands. According to a study of Klijn (1981) at the Ministry of Justice in 1980 at least 10% of the Bar (remunerates) derives its income entirely from social and welfare law cases of the poverty clientele. More than 20% of the Bar, of those who specialise in subsidised divorce cases are included.

Also Belgium universities joined the "legal aid wave" of the 1970s. An international forum at the University of Leuven in 1975 brought experiences from several countries into discussion focussing on special reference groups of legal aid such as consumer groups (*X, Jura Falconis,* 12, 4, 1976).

According to institutional traditions in Belgium the initiative for legal aid had to come from social interest groups and political parties rather than from state subsidies. Trade unions as well as local party representatives have since long offered legal advice to their clientele resp. their members; local Bar Associations had been providing pro deo advice for people without the means to pay for a lawyer. Such traditionally marginal activities were reinforced in the 1970s, special buros improving access to legal services were set up in major cities. A number of these were studied by the Antwerp Centre for Sociology of Law in a very thorough analysis of their clientele and the kinds of problems in which advice was given.

As in legal aid schemes which are run by lawyers as a complement to their regular services for paying clients, the bulk of legal aid cases asks advice in family matters (40%), mostly related to divorce, consumer problems and rental problems making up for most of the rest (18% each). The number of clients as a whole being small, we may safely conclude that these services did not basically alter the traditional supply of lawyer services. As Geerts (1977) points out, legal access in Belgium has never been a monopoly of the Bar, services for the poor have rather been supplied by interest organisations and political party buros as part of their general interest representation. A plurality of institutions offering legal advice is also the result of the Dutch development of legal aid in the 1970s. As Nils van Manen (1978) shows, public legal aid and governmental subsidies for lawyers did not render legal aid by interest group associations redundant.

Legal aid – not only in social matters, but all private legal matters, has traditionally been one of the services of the Dutch trade unions. With public legal aid the trade unions had to specialise as Niemeijer (1979) shows comparing legal aid provided by the trade unions with those of the public aid bureau in the province of Groningen. Most clients only ask for information and short advice. Legal aid offices were able to push trade union advisers out of this market wherever Legal Aid was more decentralized. Trade unions, however, retained their function of representing their members in more difficult cases, especially if invoking courts was concerned. Furthermore, community social workers have always served as referral agencies for problems, especially with public administration. Even though their services are centered around the traditional social work function, their advice always also includes assistance in legal matters. Together with legal clinics in some of the Law Schools and student volunteer services, a great variety of legal aid institutions developed in the 1970s which often competed in political and ideological approach. Together, this supply has fostered a number of innovations both in substantive as well as procedural law. A specialised advocacy for public interest groups developed. The Dutch experience shows that public legal aid did not lead to more competition for lawyer services in their traditional field of activity, but rather that it enlarged the 'legal market' by adding new forms of litigation.

But legal advice does not always lead to invoking the courts as lawyers solve their cases more often by the negotiation than by court. Thus, supporting legal aid does not foster as much 'superfluous litigation' as has been feared by many court managers.

Berghuis (1982) shows that lawyers prefer to negotiate, to phone, and to write letters rather than go to court. In almost all legal matters, negotiation 'under the shadow of the law' is the first phase before any legal procedure. It can also be considered as an attempt to avoid them. Except for divorce (where courts have to be involved), legal aid is more often spent on advice and negotiation than on pursuing litigation. However, the publicity and the supply of a different form of legal aid has certainly led many to perceive their problems in legal terms. We would therefore expect that a 'legal need' study done now would render higher scores of those who perceive 'legal problems' than the studies of 1970.

J. Griffiths has criticised this effect of legal need service in his review of "De weg naar het recht" (1977). He argues that people who do not use lawyer services should not be considered as 'incapable of satisfying their needs' but rather as taking a deliberate consumer choice. According to Griffiths, raising expectations about going to lawyers and to courts supports a deplorable trend towards juridification of everyday problems. However, after more than ten years of Legal Aid development we may state as a fact that inequality in access to courts has been reduced considerably by Legal Aid. In the early seventies, Schuyt stated that interviewees who come out perceiving more legal problems are found at both extremes of the social strata; with the self-employed at one end and recipients of social aid at the other. It turns out that the type of problems are socially specific. While the more affluent name private law problems mainly in connection with debt enforcement, low income people name problems in relation with public administration, housing rental, and labour law. As might be expected, family problems are distributed quite equally across all social strata.

The social distribution of perceived legal problems, however, does not necessarily lead to a similar distribution of plaintiffs in court. With the exception of family law, most of the plaintiffs in civil courts are businessmen and firms who are mostly suing private parties. In labour matters, it is usually the worker or employee who sues the employer. Social Security courts and procedures against administration are always invoked by private citizens, who sue an insurance or public agency.

The possibilities of bringing cases to court where the conflict rises out of aggregated collective interests is analysed in a legal dissertation integrating present day knowledge on party constellations in litigation: Groenendijk (1981) states that especially in higher courts, organizations often appear as 'parties behind the party'. Even where, formally the plaintiff is a private person, he in reality often represents some collective interest. In accordance with Galanter's theory of 'strategic advantage of the repeat players in court' he discusses those constellations of interest in which courts can be used. The procedural possibilities vary from one legal system to another. 'Amicus curae' or 'class action' found in American law, the 'action collective', in French law or the 'actio popularis' in Roman law serve similar purposes. Comparative law does not give evidence for any of the arguments against such possibilities of invoking courts as they are brought forward by Dutch lawyers. Groenendijk's dissertation demonstrates how sociological research on access to law can be related to litigation theory, and that both should give rise to revisions of procedural law restrictions to access to court. Analysis of the party constellations in different conflicts in court can give clues as to how law can effectively fulfill its function of compensating for social inequality.

That such compensation keeps courts increasingly busy can be seen in studies of two special courts which experienced a dramatic increase in their case-loads in recent years, both designed to compensate for legal problems that private citizens have with (quasi)-government agencies. They are: 1) the study of Schuyt et al. (1978) on claims against social insurance and; 2) that of Breeuwsma et al. (1982) on complaints against city or provincial administration. The relationship of the parties here is by definition unbalanced. Chances of success for the plaintiffs are very low. With some variation according to the subject matter of the complaints, chances of success range between 10% and 15%. Chances to achieve at least partial success by negotiation range around 30% on the average (with some matters they can be predicted to be as low as 5%, with a few up to 45%). Clearly, the possibilities for settlement are restricted according to the degree to which administrations are bound to strict legal regulation.

Schuyt et al. (1978) analyse the perspective of the plaintiffs. The researchers make use of the advantage of knowing the profile of all potential plaintiffs in case of a negative decision by Social Security. Thus they were able to interview a sample of complainants as well as a control group of non-complainants in similar problem constellations. However the social characteristics do not show any consistent differences to explain why some of those concerned invoked a complaint procedure and why others did not. The control group is alike according to age, occupation, income and status. Most of those who experienced some negative decisions by social insurances are in lower occupational positions. Those who go to court have consulted legal aid beforehand. It remains open, however, whether legal aid initiated that decision to complain, or whether seeking advice was only the first step. It can only be stated that in spite of poor chances of success legal aid did not prevent clients from trying (mostly hopeless) procedures.

Low success rates in Social Security Courts explain why most plaintiffs show disappointment after the procedure is over. Even when they have been present before the judge, they show a far-reaching ignorance and misunderstanding of their legal claims and the meaning of procedural activities. Explaining to lay parties takes time and efforts. Therefore, ;most judges as well as legal representatives prefer not to have the parties present. Since they have to work through heavy case-loads, they consider it better to communicate by letter than to talk to the parties in person. This holds even truer in the appelate courts. Here, procedures take place largely with the exclusion of the parties involved. This is understandable with regard to the complexity of social law, but disastrous for any attempt to gain acceptance of legal decisions.

Breeuwsma et al. (1981) analyzed a new procedure of lodging administrative complaints introduced by statutory law (AROB) in 1976. The AROB-procedure was an attempt to lower the barrier of access to the court in administrative matters on one hand, and on the other, to divert some of the increasing case-load from the highest Dutch administrative court (Raad van State). The diversion effect met with little success. The main impact of the new type of process is to simplify handling of complaints which has resulted in stimulating even more complaints. Growth rates are rising since the law was introduced six years before Breeuwsma's study was made. However, increasing proneness to file complaints cannot be causally related to the new procedure and its effect of lowering access barriers. Since the object of most of the complaints is related to construction and housing, the caseloads of complaints is also connected with increasing social pressure in a very problematic policy area. Breeuwsma et al. (1982) analysed the procedure chosen for which the AROB-law leaves a choice: small communities mostly chose a model according to which the civil servant who took the decision deals with the complaint himself. Bigger communities take the complaint to an advisory committee first which has to give a recommendation after granting formal audience to the plaintiff. Whatever diversion effect there was, it was somewhat bigger where the procedure had been formally introduced. This however, is related to a much higher rate of complaints in bigger communities. A general theory of litigation will have to conclude that 'alternative' procedures can rarely be expected to alleviate the work load of the courts, but that they rather serve to satisfy needs as yet unmet for legal complaints. What was designed as a response to curb increasing litigation has turned out to be a stimulus for even more of it.

The differentiation of legal procedures by erecting special tribunals is an international phenomenon contributing to the increase of litigation in all European countries. A Belgian study of labour relations tribunals (werkrechterraden) which look back upon a 19th century tradition (comparable to the French Prud'hommes) throws some light on the process of "judicialization" which labour relations have gone through (Langerwerf, 1982). Especially in comparison to the Dutch institutional set-up where there are no special labour tribunals, the Belgian study demonstrates with some historical depth, that the supply of legal institutions *attracts* conflicts to become litigeous which under comparable social circumstances but without that institutional supply remain largely outside judicial fora (such as labour dismissal cases which in the Netherland are handled by a preventive complaint testing procedure, thus avoiding a large number of a-posteriori conflicts).

Litigation theory: Analyses of penal procedure

Research on both civil as well as penal procedures show that the cases that get to court are only a small part of those potentially suitable. Even the case that make it to court are 'settled' more often than decided by final judgement. However, the method of selection varies considerably from one legal system to another. The English speaking reader might be surprised to learn how comparatively few civil cases in continental European courts are settled and how few penal cases are dropped or settled by pretrial conviction. In continental legal systems, rules of evidence are not as strict as in adversary trials, thus the sharp distinction of trial and non-trial procedures is unknown. Therefore, the amount of activities trying to reach settlement and the bargaining by prosecutors which tend to be out of "anglo-saxon" courts partly take place in court on the continent. This renders them less visible, they therefore hardly get to be the object of research. Jurisprudence in all cultures is mostly concerned with those procedures which lead to a decision of the court. It hardly ever looks at the selection that takes place in early stages of the procedure and that determines which cases will finally reach the courtroom. Judges usually underestimate the number of potential cases that do not reach them because lawyers find a way out of all prosecutors decide to drop the case.

Courtroom sociologists have shared this blindness for a long time. They have been observing what is easily seen in open court. They have busied themselves with theories of how judges arrive at their decisions, and they have asked themselves whether the judges fulfill the postulates of equal treatment and impartiality under the law. In the 1970s criminological research on prosecutors and on the arrest decisions of investigatory judges turned away from this traditional preoccupation with courtroom. But there is still some research to be done before the analyses of early stages of criminal investigation can be linked to those of judicial decision making (and thus before an integrated theory of penal procedure can be arrived at). In our view, this integration will have to take place in the framework of police, prosecutors, advocates, and courts forming a network of both formal and informal procedures and routines which have some cooperation intereets in common as well as perform their role bound adversary interests.

Courtroom observations hardly ever grasp the background organisation of what can be openly observed. This is due in part to the researchers not

34

only feeling some sympathy for the suspect, but also their lack of information about what is going on 'behind the scenes'. As a result of this perspective, they come up with results on how penal procedure is missing the goal of communicating court procedures to the accused. The criticism in reaction to the lack of communication in formal procedures has been formulated effectively by Hoefnagels (1970, 1980). Starting with the basic assumption that penal courts form unbalanced communication situations and that these are characterised by rituals, Hoefnagels tries to make the reader understand each of the participants' logic. He states that the adversary roles of accusing prosecutors and defending lawyers as well as the formal impartiality of judges are overruled by their common attitudes as jurists and by the fact that they are not personally involved and that they share a common interest in getting things done. Thus, adversary roles gets to be mere play which cannot hide the underlying interest in longterm cooperation. The suspect remains outside this professional communication. He has the least chance to understand its patterns and to influence its outcome. The degree to which the suspects are left out of the game is illustrated by many examples, but there is no attempt to quantify any factors that aggravate or alleviate the situation. The conclusions, therefore, remain on the level of practical suggestions: the author asks for less ritual, more common language, the suspects' right to look into their own files, and training judges in interaction. His pragmatic, almost journalistic approach, however, has been more effective in propagating reforms of penal procedure than the more strictly standardised observation study of Snel (1977). His multivariate analysis relates property crime, drunk driving, and violent crime according to suspect profiles, methods of committing crime, and behaviour in the courtroom. A distinction is made between those factors which are somehow legitimate in legal reasoning (such as age, seriousness of damage, guilty plea), and those which should not play any role (personal characteristics, interaction, behaviour). As might be expected, there remains some variance after keeping all those variables constant which have some basis in the law. Some of this variance can be explained by personality and interaction factors. However, this doesn't surprise us very much. First of all, doubt remains whether unexplained variance does not simply mirror the difficulties of finding valid indicators for some of the legal rules of procedure. But even disregarding this slight doubt, it still remains without much consequence if extra-legal factors have been discovered in legal decision making as this might be within the range of judges' discretion. Perhaps most illuminating is the uniformity of the ways in which not only legal, but also extra-legal factors are handled. The study reports exactly the same patterns of variables in decision making by the judges as by state-prosecutors. This leads to the conclusion that what is called 'extra-legal-factors' is not simply decisions at the will of individual decision makers, but that they form an 'informal programme of decision making' which is common to all of the trained lawyers involved in penal procedure.

There are quite a number of quantitative analyses of variance that evaluate whether criminal cases are charged or dropped by prosecutors. They usually work from the assumption that a main goal of procedural law is to guarantee uniform handling of legal criteria even in the investigation stage. The postulate of equal treatment should not only be applied to cases charges in court, but also to the decisions of nor charging and of dropping cases. In line with this goal is the analysis of Franken (1973). He compares all cases of drunk driving investigated by state prosecutors in 1964. On the average, 13% were not brought to court, but this rate varied considerably among the prosecutors' offices within the Netherlands. Differences in evidence explain most of the variance, thus relieving prosecution from most of the doubts about their impartiality. However, as court evidence is entirely determined by what the police have placed in the files, there remains the question why such big local differences in police inquest are tolerated. Some variance also occurs according to social characteristics of the suspects, leading to a slight bias in favor of the higher social strata irrespective of the locality where the case was pending. But this does not irritate the author so much. As the goal of his analysis is oriented toward (any kind of) uniformity of decisions, Franken mainly cares about local differences. He concludes that there should be a more centralised, computer controlled prosecution policy.

In line with such postulates, the national ministry of justice issued common guidelines for state prosecution and implemented central control of their decisions. Quantitative research has participated in controling prosecutors mainly by analysing reasons for dropping cases. It should be mentioned that publication of the prosecutor's guidelines (which had formerly been published only internally) has been a result of sociology of law publications. Hoekema (1978) stressed the quasi-legal character of these guidelines and concludes that they therefore should be published. The ministry of justice gave way to this.

Furthermore, a great deal of research by the ministry as well as by university criminologists has been devoted to decision patterns of prosecutors. The research projects of Jongman and Smale (1972, 1973) are restricted to property crimes. They relate social characteristics of the suspects as far as can be seen from the prosecutor's files with characteristics of the offence and with the decisions of prosecutors and courts. Prosecutors' discretion as well as penalty can partly be explained by social class differences: lower class members are significantly more often charged and they receive higher penalties than middle and upper class members. Predicted differences according to age, sex, or nationality were not found. The files show some of the reasoning for class differences: prior records, unemployment, and unfavourable prognoses for future behaviour correlate with class and can explain the differences. The authors conclude that these legal criteria are secondary class characteristics. Class discrimination thus is not personal bias of judges and prosecutors but it can be traced back into the criteria which are laid down by law and policy guidelines. Thus, the decision program which cause judges to look at prior record and consider prognosis factors is criticised as being inherently class biased. Some doubt remains in the discussion of this research whether these differnces could be due to the possibility that different social classes typically commit different kinds of crime. The authors therefore stress that their results have to be complemented by research using other methical approaches. Such an attempt to identify factors of prosecutional decisions using strictly comparable cases has been undertaken by a research group in the ministry of justice. Tulkens and Bergeijk (1972) presented a number of prosecutors with several fictitious cases and measured how 'mildly' or 'severely' they judged the case. Prosecutors also had to indicate which information out of the files they had used to reach their decision. However, this explained only a small part of the variance. On the whole state-prosecutors' decisions were much milder than were those of a random sample of the population as has been shown by Buikhuisen and van Dijk (1975).

The most extensive data gathering on prosecutorial policy with respect to burglary, murder, and rape has been published by Zomer (1981). In a first step of analysis they correlate characteristics of the offense and of the offenders (as far as could be seen from files) with whether the suspects have been charged and which penalties have been asked for. Since these factors could not sufficiently explain prosecutorial policy, they were complemented by a survey of three prosecutors' offices asking the prosecutors which factors they themselves think are decisive. Both studies together could very well lead to satisfactory explanations of how decisions are made in the prosecutors' office. The files here include all the information gathered by the police, plus the subsequent decision of the court. Zomer, however, was interested only in uniformity of charging and pleading policy. Thus he restricts himself to recommendations on how the ministry could increase central control, rather than contributing to explanatory theory on why prosecutors often differ.

The publications of the research department of the Ministry of Justice unfortunately give scarce descriptive information. Often, they only report correlation coefficient. The reader, especially the non-social-science reader, thus misses much of the information which could be useful to legal policy discourse. The opposite is true of ethno-methodological studies of Frid (1982) of the investigate judge which gives very good descriptions, but unfortunately very few theoretical analysis: Fird's participant observation and non-standardised interviews show the formal as well as informal work organisation of all of those who participate in decisions on arrests and on whether suspects should stay in prison before trial. Formal law only provides a basic outline for the 'real organisation' which depends on the work-patterns of policeagents, the reinterpretation of testimony by interpreters for foreign suspects, and the decisions which, formally, only deal with whether and under what conditions the suspect should stay under arrest. All of these factors determine what information the investigative judge will get and how he disposes of a case. The reader can conclude from the narrative descriptions how common sense understanding of crime is transformed into legal terms. It may serve as a warning that the interests of routine and of getting work done dominates especially at the end of the day and before weekends. Lawyers are also involved in this informal organisation adjusting their advocatary principles to common workgroup interests. Lawyers have to take into consideration the expectations of other forensic team players as well as those of their clients. This restricts advocatary possibilities in the pretrial state. The best that any of the participants can do in the interest of a suspect would be to make the procedure as transparent and understandable as possible. Especially the division of labor between investigations at the police, at the prosecutors' office, the role of investigative judges, and of the final day in court seem largely incomprehensible to the suspects. This prevents suspects from behaving competently.

The Dutch penal organisation provides for social workers who are required to give some legal counsel as well as social aid to anybody put under arrest. However they come into the picture 24 hours after the arrest has taken place which in most cases is to late to give any legal counsel, but only just manages to help with some of the social consequences of the arrest (Tigges/Nuijten-Edelbruch, 1981).

More important for legal defense is a law passed in 1957 which provides a lawyer for anyone as soon as they are arrested. The bar has helped to arrange immediate service especially during the night and over weekends. Criminological research by Bergsma (1977) has helped to establish this service and later to evaluate it. As the author has been involved in formulating the law, his evaluation is restricted to its original goals. A more critical report comes from the ministry of justice which relates arrest to later decisions in penal procedure: The report of Berghuis and Tigges (1981) demonstrates differences in styles of control between the comparatively 'unruly' Amsterdam with The Hague which shows less criminal density. While under Amsterdam's work pressure, arrest has been used as a pretrial sanction outside of formal law (with the expectation that the courts will later legitimise the arrest with a prison sentence), there is much more judicial control of arrest-decisions in The Hague at the price of not having immediate intimidating and sanctioning possibilities.

We cannot report on all the research done on pretrial penal procedures. Our examples show that there is ample evaluation, especially by governmental research. It is remarkable that most of it involves looking at decisions to prosecute, and that courtroom study has been done only by university researchers. Analyses seems to be directed at central control and uniformity more than at efficiency or due process. University research, however, has largely identified with the perspective of the suspect.

Lack of research: The court procedures per se

It seems like a paradox: researching the context of legal aid usually presupposes that barriers to access have to be lowered in order to achieve equal treatment in court. This as well as research on prosecutors has applied the postulate of equal treatment not only to decision by the court, but also to the conditions before the court procedure. Basically, they conclude that there should be less discretion in dropping cases. They imply as a consequence that more cases get into court. Access barriers are to be lowered and discretion is to be reduced. Penal procedural equality does not argue for decriminalising petty and aggressive crimes, but rather to criminalise white collar crime, environmental pollution, etc.

Courtroom observations, on the other hand, show that legal procedure has only a limited capacity for solving social conflicts. Hypotheses on extra-legal factors in judicial decision making could question its impartiality. But they turn out to be less realistic than expected, especially if inherent class bias of substantive law is disregarded. Thus, the critique of social science research turns to the formality of procedures, to its routines and rituals which prevent communication. They 'take away' the underlying social conflict from suspects as well as victims. Not class bias, but 'judicial alieniation' becomes the main point of critique.

Procedural reforms could hardly do away with such deficits. They could marginally improve communication in the courtroom, but they could not deny that legal decisions are always direct against the interests of at least one of the parties concerned. This implies that the relationship of the participants varies with social distance and that their behaviour is governed by their desire to win. Judges on the other hand have to demonstrate impartiality and firmness. Therefore their deliberation takes place backstage. Procedural reform ideas which regard the penal process as a 'conflict solving' situation as well as those which are directed at improving its efficiency, have to take into consideration that one of the functions of courts is symbolic presentation of legitimacy. Dutch procedural research has yet to discover courts as a workorganisation. Lack of regard to organisational factors is also apparent in psychological research in the tradition of the 'theory of judicial argumentation' trying to reconstruct decisions of judges with the help of models of rational behaviour: In the very very clear presentation of the psychology of problem solving by Crombag et al. (1977) processes, many of the illusions and contradictions of the methodology of jurisprudence are laid out. Psychological analysis stresses the role of common sense presupposition. It describes judicial rationality as largely argumentation *after* the decision, which is not so much directed at arriving at decisions, but rather at legitimising them. But, their models assume rationality. They never include the social conditions under which judges work and under which they are educated. Rationality models usually do not take into consideration that the decisions in the courtroom do not take place only in the head of judges, but that they develop in the course of interaction between advocates, parties, and witnesses. Thus, the analysis seems capable of giving a rational critique of judicial argument, but it gives no explanation on how judicial process actually takes place.

An attempt to get closer to the reality of judicial decision making is made by Ten Kate and Van Koppen (1982) with their psychological-empirical research using the method of fictitious cases: 114 Judges had to decide on nine fictitious graded according to factorial dimensions such as 'social compensatory' versus 'legalistic' versus 'publiscitarian' values. Control groups of lay-persons and law students are taken for comparison. The analysis comes up with a great variance of answers, but hardly any consistent pattern which could explain them. That is to say: knowledge of prior decisions can hardly predict future ones. Expected correlations with biographical data and personality characteristics do not hold. The best explanation can be found in role attitudes of the judges: whether they are 'legalistic' or 'socially' oriented or oriented at 'individual moral values'. The authors interpret their results largely as falsification of original hypotheses, but some doubt remains whether or not they could simply be an indicator for the lack of validity in measurement. As the study very carefully considers all measurement problems, we might, for the time being, regard it as a result that personality characteristics do not largely influence the decision making behavior of judges. The demonstrated relationship between role understanding and decision making could be interpreted as a sign of consistency in self-understanding. Judges do realise that the public expects their decision to be strictly bound by law while they themselves stress their discretion. Future research will have to start out with the results of this study that role perception of judges does not necessarily lead to valid conclusions on their decision-making behavior.

If psychological research moves from rational models of judicial decision-making in the direction of more empirical information on actual behaviour, there is none of this to be found in analyses of judicial decisions, such as the dissertation of Snijders (1978). He gives a full report of the types of arguments which have been used in decisions of the highest Appelate Court from 1970-1974 and in a representative sample of decisions of Higher Court in 1973. It mirrors quantitatively the reasoning in judicial argumentation; it should therefore not come as a surprise that the author finds some legal rule under which each of the decisions can fall. He concludes that, in judicial decisionmaking there is no space for 'irrationalities'. Confronted with such a inference we can only reiterate that the function of legal argumentation is not to present the motives for decisionmaking, but rather to give reasons legitimising decisions before an appelate court. It should therefore be interesting to see how such legal reasoning can be contradicted and altered in appelate decisions while nevertheless presenting judicial arguments as consistent. The quantitative evaluation shows that this pretention or consistency is achieved. In order to explain how this is done, however, the study should have gone more into the substance of argumentation topoi such as they were used in the study. There are methodological reasons why the substance of judicial argumentation is hard to quantify. Ten Kate/Van Koppen (supra) state with some surprise that judges and lay-interviewees largely agree in their decisions. They conclude that judicial reasoning is largely 'hindsight argumentation' which tries to give legitimisation to decision outcomes which have been arrived at using common sense.

Nevertheless, the observable influence of lay-judges on the bench seems small as Roos (1982) demonstrates. There is no jury and there are few lay-judges in Dutch courts. Social insurance courts (Raden van Beroep) form an exception. Lay-judges here are experts representing trade unions on one side, and employers on the other. But these lay-judges hardly ever take an active role in the courtroom. Also, behind the scenes, they largely follow the opinions given by professional judges. Lay-judges seem especially concerned about demonstrating their impartiality. When a decision seemed very one-sided, the experts tried to push in the direction of a middle position, thus acting in contradiction to the expected tendency of representing only their interest group. On the whole, Roos documents that the lay-judges are more concerned about demonstrating their impartiality than at influencing decisions. This is confirmed in interviews of the professional judges, while the lay-judges give a much more optimistic picture of their influence. According to Roos the main function of lay-judges in social insurance courts is to increase their legitimacy within their interest groups. At the same time, they remain free to criticise social law in the legislative arena, since in appelate courts there is no lay-representation in social insurance cases.

Concluding remarks

Social science procedural research contributes to better understanding the transformation of conflicts when entering legal procedure. Sociological research often criticises from the perspective of those who have to subdue to legal procedure. In doing so, the standards of 'due process' or 'strict impartiality' often are applied, not so much because sociologists would regard these as the only criteria for evaluating judicial procedure, but because these are the ones they can most legitimately communicate to a lawyer audience. In addition social science has formulated it own standards such as 'public access to procedure in all stages' and 'maximising' communication and transparency'. None of these might be satisfactorily reached, but they should nevertheless be strived for. But social science research also points at the limit of improving legal procedure. It can (and should) more clearly state under which conditions judicial procedure is incapable of handling problems and should therefore be avoided.

It should be one of the goals of legal sociology to show which conflicts are not suited for legal decision-making and which should better be handled by another type of institution. Elements of such 'alternatives to judicial procedure' can even be found in the forms of bargaining, and compromise. Research on procedure in private law, penal law, and administrative law uniformly shows that there are numerous ways out of legal procedures before a final decision has to be reached.

Dutch and Flemish sociology of law has contributed to such insights by concentrating on procedural stages before entering court. Mostly it has done this by looking at barriers to access and at the selectivity of entry into judicial procedures. Research, so far, seems to me insufficient concerning the patterns of procedures themselves; especially the many methods of avoiding escalation into more formal stages of process. This will only be achieved by looking more closely at the different ways of handling and ending court procedures. One would be able to show that there is as much selectivity within the procedure as there is before entering. This could very well turn out to be an important contribution to the recent discussion on how to reduce the costs of the judiciary.

A necessary step for the analysis of the increase of litigation in recent years and the growth of the legal profession will be to form indicators for the degree of litigeousness in different areas of conflict such as the amount of penal cases in traditional areas of crime (like theft or injury) compared to modern forms of crime (like organized white collar crime, environmental pollution or the mass phenomena of traffic violations keeping penal courts busy), the amount of traditional civil cases (like debt enforcement) as compared to modern issues of litigation which are predominantly cases against public administration (complaints against taxation, against social services, housing administration and city planning). Historical trend analyses of litigation rates (Van Houtte, Langerwerf, 1977; Langerwerf 1978) in Belgium, show that a relationship between rising court caseloads and industrialisation holds for the 19th century alone, in the first half of the 20th century many litigation figures have been amazingly constant. Recent growth in litigation rates has been concomitant with economic stagnation more than with economic growth. Considering the kinds of issues which keep courts increasingly busy, we should warn against any causal links that might be maintained between the rise of legal aid and increasing case loads: it rather looks as if the increase of litigation as well as the increasing demand for legal aid can be traced back to common causal factors in societal change such as urbanization, more social mobility in family as well as working relations, increasing governmental regulation and complaints arising from higher levels of expectation and participation. There is every reason to integrate the quantitative analysis of litigation indicators with the qualitative concerns of improving the responsiveness of legal procedures.

The socio-legal approach to the institutes of family law: Trend report

J. VAN HOUTTE and C. COZIJN

Socio-legal research is conducted in Belgium by the Centre of Sociology of Law (University of Antwerp – UFSIA) and in the Netherlands by the Research and Documentation Centre of the Ministry of Justice.

A. Sociological research on family law at the Centre of Sociology of Law (University of Antwerp – UFSIA)

J. VAN HOUTTE

When comparing the general situation of sociology of law in Belgium with the Netherlands, the comparison turns out in favour of the Netherlands. With regard to research on the institutes of family law, however, equally much is found in both countries, or to put it differently, equally little. What is true for Belgium and the Netherlands holds, "mutatis mutandis", for the other countries.

Why is there so little interest on the part of sociology of law in the institutes of family law?

Within the legal-sociological area itself little room is left for the social-scientific approach to family law. There may be difficulties associated with the specific legal-sociological side of such an approach. When one speaks about the rule of law or the administration of justice, the legal-sociological focus appears to be obvious and unproblematic. The nucleus of the legal system has been touched. But in the case of the institutes of family law the situation is not the same. One seems to practice sociology of the family, rather than sociology of law. An explanation herefor lies in the fact that the relation marriage, household and family is problematic.

Another reason why the family institutes are treated in a stepmotherly fashion within the sociology of law, has probably to do with its latent socially problematic character. Criminality, important and even small, comes, thanks to the media, on the public forum. In a society in which the state of prosperity and wellbeing are being held as an ideal and continuously attract the interest as a subject of discussion, the effectuation of granted right will easily be taken into account. In the prolongation then lies the entrance into the law court. Marriage and family problems and especially the problematic juridical superstructure appear less as a crucial issue.

As a consequence it is not astonishing that the authorities show only a moderate interest in it. Although parliament and the minister of justice recognize the need for reforms in the sphere of family law, matters are quietly permitted to take their own routine course. The traditional "experts" proceed dogmatically. If necessary, the ideological side really comes into discussion. Nevertheless, every day reality, which does not announce itself forcefully, is left aside. The need to set up an inquiry is less apparent here, because the concerned categories are not institutionalized and have no politically mighty spokesmen: e.g. parents in need entitled to support, women entitled to support, adoptable children, housewives who experience little the legal equality to their husbands.

The problematic side of the legal sociological angle of incidence and the hidden socially problematic character of the matter are for us exhortations and legitimize setting up legal-sociological research on the institutes of family law.

A legal-sociological angle of incidence

Possible paradigms regarding the relation between the law and the reality of the family are a starting-point. As a rule, it is assumed that the law lags behind social evolution in this matter. The fact that the law is used to direct the status of the family is less emphasized.

On the basis of the first paradigm two research topics can be formulated in view of the fact that whether or not a law reform has taken place.

In the first case, the question arises to which extent the prevailing legal institute is socially alienated? In this context two subordinate questions may be formulated: into the social (in)effectiveness on the one hand, and into the socio-cultural (in)adequacy on the other hand.

Institutes of the family law want to give form to definite values and want, moreover, to offer solution mechanisms for conflicts between the concerned parties. Through the study of their working the *effectiveness* can be sounded. Have the objectives of the legislator been realized? While studying the (in)adequacy, the legal institute as such is put into question. Belgian family law rules to a large extent sometimes go back to the time of the "Code Civil" (1804). The legislator of that time created them to find a solution for definite social needs. He did so from a personal time-related perspective and tried to link up with the values and the structure of time, as he perceived them. After more than 175 years the social values and structures will probably have changed noticeably. Do the then created rules fit into the socio-cultural system of today? Which changes in the social value systems and which changes in the structures possibly affect them?

Following a law reform the research question may be formulated somewhat differently. Can it really be termed a catching-up manoeuvre? Had the legal institute lagged behind with regard to the reality of the family? If so, has the law reform reduced or even done away with the discrepancy?

Although less common, the paradigm "social engineering" deserves to serve as a starting-point for legal-sociological research in the domain of family law. Why should it be excluded 'a priori' that family law rules are used to direct or to start evolution in social reality?

From a social-problematic starting-point to a policy-directed conclusion

We think that at the origin of every sociological research there has to be a social problem. This problem must be clearly explained at the start of the research. In this way one prevents sociological research from coming across as "socially alienated" and it is made easier to come to policy conclusions at the end of the research. As the survey of the research of the Centre of Sociology of Law (UFSIA – Antwerp) shows, such social problems have been defined for each research: the aged in need, who in the welfare state want to appeal to the community and are relegated to family solidarity: the ever growing number of divorced women who, for their security of subsistence, depend on the (un)willing ex-husbands; adoptable children who apparently do not get adopted, although the legislator carried through "ad hoc" lawreforms; questions about the real emancipation of the married woman after the legal equalization of man and woman in patrimonial matters.

In conclusion of the research one should always pay careful attention to policy conclusions. Objections to this come from two opposite sides. Supporters of an engaged sociology, where values, facts and actions are not separated, will point to the contradiction between the objectivating ethos, which is proper to us, and the value-bound character of policy conclusions. From the other side of the management the same contradiction is pointed out. We are reproached with border transgression. To this we reply that even for the supporter of an objectivating sociology, which wants to maintain a distinction between conscience and science, it nevertheless appears to be not only justified, but even necessary to formulate policy conclusions. Their formulation takes however place under well-defined conditions. The policy conclusions will always be formulated in a separate final chapter. The empirical and evaluation elements as such are also to be carefully indicated. If different value orientations lead to different conclusions, then this should be mentioned. Possibly there is a choice in favour of one solution, but then the adhered-to value orientation ought to be clearly indicated.

Under these conditions a lot speaks strongly in favour of policy conclusions to be drawn by the researchers. They have a thorough knowledge of the problems. Moreover, the transfer to the management is facilitated. Statesmen appear to have difficulties recognizing relevance of the results published as such to the management and drawing themselves policy conclusions from them. If the researcher himself formulates policy conclusions, then the relevance to management has been indicated and possible conclusions are stated. However, it is the task of the management to outline and apply to chosen policy.

Obsolete institutes of family law?

The maintenance obligation intends to guarantees a minimum means of existence by appealing to family ties. Now that the latter are losing their significance, it is, of course, being questioned. In order to arrive at valid conclusions, it is indicated to compare the concrete variants of the obligation to support with the specific social context. Thus, we studied successively the obligation to support between children and their aged parents on the one hand, and the obligation to support between ex-spouses on the other hand.

Elderly persons in need and children liable for their maintenance[1]

A sociological review of law practices in Public Assistance Agencies and Justice of the Peace Courts. Some ten years ago, the problems of the aged were discovered. Their weak economic status is one of these points. So the question arises who is financially liable for the aged. The community at large has taken a large part of the burden but the maintenance obligation of the children remains in force.

In order to construct an empirical picture of the maintenance of the aged by their adult children, we employed various sources of information. For historical perspective, we inquired into changes in the content of substantive rules, their origin, the intention of the legislators, and the cultural context in which they were enacted. We also studied how the Code Napoleon had been interpreted by analyzing published judgments. We examined the current application of these rules by analysing records of the P(ublic) A(ssistance) A(gencies) of the city of Antwerp (309 maintenance records from 1969) and judgments of 13 Judges of the Peace of the district of Antwerp and by interviewing officials (judges, lawyers, administrators and social workers of the P.A.A.).

Before analyzing the present operation of the institute, we shall outline in a first part its historical relativity. We investigated the historical stages of the maintenance obligations in connection with the family solidarity structures and means of subsistence. In Roman society, the extended family structures gradually disappeared and a kind of nuclear family became dominant. The emperor interfered in the second century after Christ and he provided legal claims for obtaining primary aid. In the Middle Ages we could demonstrate

[1]   Cfr. Van Houtte, Breda 76; idem 1978.

that a similar transition has taken place. In particular since the 15th century, family communities in our country were on the decrease and the moral obligation was legalized.

Our current law originated with the French Civil Code. The Institute of maintenance obligation was drafted in a "status-related" way. The aged had a right to an income related to their former wealth and to be provided by their descendants. On the basis of an analysis of published jurisdiction we have been able to show that judges until about 1880 shared the same bourgeois concerns, by taking status into account when granting maintenance. From 1880 onwards the amounts granted appear to have been more related to the minimum of existence. After the Second World War we find exclusively cases relating to this minimum. Since then a number of claims have been introduced in the courts by Public Assistance Agencies.

Our research in a second part is focused on *the problematic application of maintenance* in its coercive form.

The *first question* arising here is with regard to the efficacy of the legal institute. Are the minimum means of existence of the aged parents guaranteed by the maintenance obligation?

The main application is found in the mentioned Public Assistance Agencies (P.A.A.), where we found that 1,5 percent of the aged received money via the maintenance obligation. It appears from our survey that the ascendants were very old people, mostly unattached (widows, people divorced legally or in fact). Two thirds of the total group consists of women and half of the group are physically handicapped, all of them have very low incomes. The P.A.A. provides for 30 percent and the family gaves some 10 percent of total necessary income of the aged. The descendants, however, are thus taxed according to their incomes and do not have to answer for just any sum the ascendant is short of. Anyway, even if our survey shows that the descendant group considered has an income position reflecting the national average, it is never possible for these people to support their ascendants completely. Hence the important role of the P.A.A. in assisting these needy ascendants. This shows that the share of the descendant in supplementing the income in order to arrive at the minimum of existence, is marginal.

The *second question*, which we tried to answer, was related to the inadequacy of the legal institute. Does it still fit into the present-day socio-cultural system?

Today, sociological surveys show that the mutual solidarity between parents and children is still a concrete reality, although regular financial help seldom occurs. This means that payment of allowances is no longer practised.

The interviews showed that ascendants do not demand maintenance from their descendants. Their problems are brought into the P.A.A. and the courts usually after a series of family problems. Even after the decision, transfers of the money do not progress smoothly.

Despite all this, judges and lawyers appear to maintain the law. In the social workers' opinion the maintenance rule in the P.A.A. might best be abolished or only made to apply to extremely wealthy descendants. The P.A.A. board finally takes a rather pragmatic point of view. Abolition would certainly have positive results but there are mainly fears of a greater rush of clients.

As a conclusion, we can state that the concrete legal form is no longer adequate. Especially the automatic character of its application should be questioned. We propose that the judge should have a right of appreciation so that he no longer should be obliged to grant maintenance automatically.

We also conclude that the P.A.A.'s right of regress should be abolished and that the social problems posed there should be solved within the framework of social policy (old age care, public health services).

The maintenance obligation between husband and wife[2]

There is an increase in divorce rates and even increasing numbers of people who face problems with regard to alimony payments. This justifies yet the socio-legal attention to the institution of "obligation to provide maintenance" after divorce.

We applied three methods of investigation:
- observation of law proceedings in three courts (62 hearings were observed and 120 warrants were recorded during the month of May 1973)
- A public opinion study through a representative random sample of the Belgian population (1569 persons)
- interviewing of privileged respondents (non-representative sample of ex-spouses, magistrates and lawyers).

By means of this methods we are able to answer the basic questions of our study.

[2]   Cfr. De Vocht, Verhoeven, Van Houtte, 1978; Van Houtte, De Vocht, 1981.

a. Is the legal institution of obligation to provide maintenance efficient towards the alimony-entitled woman?

There are several indications that the ex-wife, who in our socio-cultural context is the alimony-entitled party, is not helped adequately.

1. Firstly it is obvious that the awarded alimonies are not sufficient.
2. The judicial settlement of the alimony conflicts is problematic.
3. The payment of alimony is irregular.

b. Is the regulation of maintenance obligation contested?

There are different arguments for this. Individualization of marriage puts the fault-based granting of alimony into question. The development towards equal partner relationships can question the concept of alimentary obligation as such. The revision of the legislative matter on maintenance between ex-spouses is under way in a number of European countries.

1. What does the public think?

By using a public opinion study we attempted to find out to which degrees the current legal regulations fit in with the existing value perceptions of the Belgian population. A very large number of respondents (84%) take into account exclusively or at a safe degree, the principe of fault. Therefore the alimony takes on a sanctioned character. Most of these respondents, or 46% are in concordance with the law, which makes both criteria (need and fault) prerequisite to the awarding of alimony. But is it not surprising that there are 498 respondents, or 38%, who only pay attention to the innocence aspect to determine alimony – and thus show even more accordance with sanctioning than the law?

If there is no contrast between the fundamental principle of the legal regulation under study and the norms of the large majority of the people, this does not mean that the whole content of the legal regulation corresponds with the opinions of the average citizen.

By taking a large number of elements of the legal practice into account, it is possible to draw more subtle conclusions. Public opinion disagrees with some elements of the legal practice. A fairly important part, about one fourth, prefers alimony limited to 5 years. In this case alimony is considered a transitory measure. In contrast to legal practice, a large majority of respondents (74%) does not want to take the social class of the involved into account. Alimony should be linked with the minimum standard of living, not with the level of affluence of the social class.

2. What are the opinions of the directly involved?

Many divorcees experience the link of alimony with fault as problematic. But this does not mean that the principle of fault was rejected by all respondents. Individuals who divorced on grounds of specific facts, receiving alimony on the basis of fault, mostly believe in the named principle.

Magistrates think positionally and thus conform to the law. They adhere mostly to legally determined criteria, fault and need. Non-magistrates stress that alimony must be paid according to need. They wish to make the principle of fault relative.

From the policy making point of view, a number of problems can be indicated which need to be resolved through future legislation: the inadequacy of the awarded amounts, the working of justice and the irregular payment of the awarded alimony.

Lawmakers in several countries are confronted with the same problems. For these problems we worked out some solutions.

Succesful law reform? Right and duties between spouses[3]

The 14th of July 1976 had to be a great day for Belgian women. On this date the new law concerning the rights and duties of spouses eliminated the last vestiges of male dominance in Belgian marriage legislation enacting total equality between the spouses. Thus the legislator hoped to make up for the lag that the law had incurred with relation to developments in the social reality. On the basis of factual knowledge the situation did not appear so simple and unequivocal. Therefore we wished to investigate in what way the equality pattern designed by the law-maker also exists in the everyday practice of the modal Belgian family. More specifically we decided to focus our research on the most innovating element in the 1976 legislation: the patrimonial equality between spouses. So our attention went to the mechanisms which make this equality possible: the principle of autonomy and the principle of "parallelism".

Autonomy standards offer husband and wife the possibility of acting without the agreement of the other spouse. So each marriage partner has the freedom of occupation, the right to collect and spend his/her own earnings, to open a bank or savings-bank account, to lease a safe and the right to

[3]   Gysels, Vogels, 1982; Gysels, Van Houtte, Vogels, 1984.

autonomous management of the personal property. The principle of parallelism, which regulates the management of communal property offers the spouses all freedom in management mode: either the husband assumes the management for his account, or the wife; nothing, however, impedes the spouses from acting jointly or alternately.

In order to make the central issue of this project researchable we needed to operationalize these patrimonial standards within the context of a concrete marriage relationship, which is not an easy task. A sample of 500 married women between the ages of 20 and 60, and living in the Dutch speaking part of Belgium (the Flemish region) have been interviewed. The results were analyzed in the following five main themes:

1. The freedom of occupation
2. The accessibility to family income
3. The spending of the family income
4. The management of personal and communal property
5. The patrimonial expedients: bank account, savings-bank account and safe.

The tendency to the legally viewed equality, equilibrium certainly lives among Flemish married couples. For the two mechanisms – autonomy and parallelism – this equilibrium is achieved in a quite different way. Concerning the autonomy standards the majority of the wives use their recently adjudged rights to autonomy and make up the delay to their husbands. Rarely is this autonomous behavior of the wife the expression of a conscious striving for autonomy. Concerning the principle of parallelism the equilibrium is achieved by the majority of couples because the broad management of communal property becomes a matter of husband and wife and not so much because the wife at certain grounds pulls the absolute power to herself. One can also notice that the equilibrium at this point is more pronounced for decision-making than it is for execution.

At the explanatory level we noticed that the legally viewed equality model has the greatest chance to exist in the everyday practice of the spouses in a rather young relationship, of which the wife has an occupational activity, a passable high educational level, a modern attitude and in which the husband has a rather high occupational level.

The draw picture seems to correspond with the new middle class salaried group.

Social engineering? The new adoption legislation[4]

In view of a revised youth protection policy the legislator wished to integrate as many as possible abandoned Belgian children into families. Adoption appeared an appropriate means thereto. Has the adoption institution not been very successful over the last decades? In 1945 563 adoptions were registered, in 1968 the annual number reached 1906. With the law of March 21st 1969, whose main objective was to promote the integration of abandoned Belgian children into families, the legislator intended to accelerate this trend. The 3479 adoptions counted in 1978 could be interpreted as if the legal interventions had actually been realized. However, there were indications that the success was only apparent.

Empirical data were collected by means of file analyses (2439 files in three courts under the jurisdiction of the Court of Appeal of Antwerp). We also interviewed 201 adoptive families. These interviews provide the research project with more indepth information.

The collected material permitted us to achieve a social and legally relevant description of the adoption institution. The ineffectiveness of the adoption law appears as a main feature towards abandoned youth. Adoption is a flag that covers three cargoes. Given the large attention paid to hetero-family adoption (charitable adoptions), one almost seems to forget the existence of regularized[5] and endo-family adoptions.[6] Most people are not aware of the fact that hetero-family adoptions represent only a minority (34%), compared with regularized (45%) and endo-family (21%) adoptions. There is more. Between 1972 and 1976 the absolute number of hetero-family adoptions declined, as well s their share in the total adoption package. Besides, hetero-family adoptions involve more and more non-Belgian children. The socially handicapped, a category of adoptable children explicitly concerned by the law, are not at all involved in the adoption process. As the adoptants are no longer required to be childless, a new category of adoptive parents appeared recently: adoptants with children of their own who prefer adoptive children of a foreign nationality.

A sociological explanatory model was designed to explain the gap between

[4]   Berckmans, De Vocht, Van Houtte, 1981; Van Houtte, 1982.
[5]   It concerns adoptions of children who are not legal, because they are born outside marriage.
[6]   It concerns adoptions within a family relation (e.g. the husband adopts a child from a previous marriage of his wife).

adoption law and adoption reality. The number of hetero-family adoptions no longer increases as they have to be realized within a specific adoption market. The blockade of the adoption market can be viewed from two angles: offer and demand. We will discuss both, considering that in our socio-legal study mainly the demand was investigated.

The offer: The adoptable children
The decline in the number of very young adoptable children is the result of general social trends. The number of unwanted pregnancies decreases because of contra-conceptive practices and abortion. Also there is a tendency for unmarried mothers to bring up their children themselves. Nevertheless, a large number of abandoned and/or neglected children are deprived of "normal" family life. These children live in institutions or with foster-parents. Not all these children qualify for adoption. There are legal as well as factual barriers.

The judge can pronounce the adoption of long-term placed children, over which the parents have parental authority, in favour of the child, against the will of the parents. However, judges seem to hesitate to pronounce an irrevocable adoption.

The adoptability of long-term placed children is not only obstructed by the above-mentioned legal barriers. Institutions allegedly restrict the potential adoption of children placed in their care or at least pursue no active adoption policy. Foster-parents on the contrary allegedly are more adoption-minded, but are restricted by legal barriers.

The demand: The adoptants
The demand was studied by means of the successful demand: people who succeed in adopting. At the start of this socio-legal study we supposed that the adoptants, as a social category, would dominate the adoption market. The term "adoptant-dominance" refers to a situation in which the adoptants refuse a part of the adoption offer because it does not answer their aspirations to form a model family. They would strive for optimal imitation of biological descent. Only very young, physically and psychologically healthy children with a minimum of ties of descent would be taken into consideration by the adoptants.

Our research results do not permit to conclude the overt dominance of the adoptants as a sociological category. The imitation of biological descent seems to be the priority purpose of the hetero-family adoptants. So the adoption of Belgian children is primarily motivated in terms of the own childlessness while the adoption of foreign children is based on more child-entered motivations. Whereas usually young children are adopted by preference, foreign children may be older. However, the fact that adoptants show a great flexibility towards the adoption market with regard to the selection criteria, contradicts the adoptant-dominance.

As far as policy is concerned, the research led to the following conclusions. New legislative initiatives have been taken to change the adoption legislation. These will perhaps bring about little practical results. If one wants a solution to the problem of the abandoned youth with the help of the adoption institute, an adoption policy should be developed that makes the adoption market function better. It should be tried to enlarge the offer by facilitating the entry to the quality of adoptable child. Besides the candidate-adoptants must be stimulated to adopt also "difficultly adoptable children". Such an adoption policy would perhaps offer a solution to the desertion of a number of children.

Nevertheless, the solution value of the adoption institute for the problems of youth protection remains restricted.

Perspectives

After the Centre of Sociology of Law had X-rayed a number of institutes of family law, it was decided that it was time for a synthesis and reflection. The Fund of Collective Scientific Research granted a credit for a project "Family and Law (court)". Up to now the relation between the two has been considered rather simplistic. The law is always behind the mores. We want to try to unravel and delineate the relations in their full complexity; in other words, to look for the different possible paradigms within the different spheres of family law. We want to react not only against the simplism of unilaterally conceived relation between law and family reality, but also against the simplism that supposes something to exist as "the present-day family". Hereby it is neglected that pluralism within the family reality has certainly not diminished in comparison to former times.

Thanks to the preceding research work the Centre seems to be well equipped to bring the project "Family and law (court)" to a good end. The paradigmatic synthesis, result of the project, would possibly form a basis for a new approach and further studying of the institutes of family law. At that moment it would also be advisable that a bridge should be built to social policy. Translated towards Belgian structures a cooperative relation should be worked out, in which are included the Department of Justice, competent for the preliminary legal work for family law, and the Community Minister of Welfare and Family. With recent experiences in mind, we fear such a cooperation will not be easily worked out. But man lives by hope.

B. Research in the sociology of law, especially on family law, at the Research and Documentation Centre of the Ministry of Justice in the Netherlands

C. COZIJN

Sociology of Law is at the Research and Documentation Centre (RDC) a relatively new field of activity. Nowadays, as well as in the past, most of the research effort is devoted to the field of criminology. During the late sixties and the early seventies government felt a growing need of help from the social sciences in order to place their policies on more solid foundations. This caused an almost explosive growth of the RDC. This expansion made it possible to devote attention to other issues than the traditional ones that criminologists are studying. Starting with victimless crimes, one paid at last attention to non-crime-phenomena. One of the first uneasy steps consisted of a research project on the relation between copying documents in the age of xerographia and the (non-)payment of copyrights. As in most instances of newly explored research fields factfinding was more the issue than the explanation of the facts found.

Perhaps the same factors that caused governments increasing need for social science knowledge have led to rapid changes in the attitudes towards the ways people should behave to one another. So in the western countries developed a movement to racial and sexual liberation and emancipation. And it will go almost without saying that these different looks on the relation between people would lead to an other way of organizing community. Family is no longer the basic principle of society and disintegration and dissolution of marriage became, though merely tolerated more or less common phenomena in our surroundings. Not only the instable marriages showed an altering attitude towards the way husbands and wives should relate to one another: the traditional sex-role differentiation in family and society grew more and more questionable. These developments made several aspects of family law increasingly contested. Having that great research potential at the RDC it was obvious that the RDC should be engaged in research related with the developments mentioned hereabove. So the research effort of the RDC in the sociology of family law had been born.

Research projects in the field of family law in the past and present

Research into the attitudes to the distribution of estate under the law of intestacy (C. Cozijn, 1978a)

Background
Research in the field of family law at the RDC started with an inquiry into the attitudes towards the distribution of estate under the law of intestacy, especially with regards to the hereditary position of the surviving spouse.

Parliamentary discussion of the Bill to amend the law on intestacy (parliamentary paper 12863 no. 2, 1974) showed wide differences in the attitudes of members as to how greatly the hereditary position of the surviving spouse should be improved as against that of the children. Such an improvement was of course considered necessary in order to get a more equitable mutual delimitation of these positions. This being so, it was decided to determine by means of an opinion survey what people thought about the law on intestacy. The object of the survey on the one hand was to determine whether any need was felt for proceeding with a change of the law in this field and, on the other, what such an amendment should consists of; in other words, what direction such a change should take. To obtain an answer to these queries, it was decided to hold oral interviews with a sample of the Dutch population. Whether a change in the law was desirable, we tried to answer from two sides. First of all, by asking about the advantages and disadvantages, if any, of the present provisions and whether those questioned, had made a will and why they had done so.

As to the substance of the change, we tried to answer this by asking the respondents to arrange four alternatives covering intestacy in order of preference. Some explanation was then given of the alternatives, in which reference was made chiefly to the consequences. Then again one was asked to arrange the alternatives by preference.

The results

Some 45% of those questioned had objections against the present hereditary position on death, as against 42% who had none. More than half of the objections raised as most important were directed towards the weak position of the surviving spouse (55%). Ten percent of the respondents had made a will. Of these, 54% had complaints about the present law of succession. With this group too most of the objections were directed against the weak position of the surviving spouse.

In addition to the existing law of succession and "everything to the survivor" three variations were proposed for a system where the surviving spouse receives at least a subsistence payment from the estate. When first presented with the alternatives, 44% opted for the principle of "everything to the survivor", 33% for the subsistence scheme, and only 19% preferred the present arrangements. After several of the consequences of the various alternatives had been explained, 36% opted for the alternative with the surviving spouse receiving a maintenance payment charged to the estate. The other alternatives has apparently lost much of their original attraction. Under this alternative, the surplus if any is divided among the children on the understanding that the children cannot inherit property but only a proportion of the value of the estate after deducting the subsistence payments. Payment of the cash sum can be demanded only after both spouses have died.

In conclusion we can say, that the survey provided three clear indications that the vast majority of the population rejects the present arrangements for intestacy. It has also become clear that criticism is directed chiefly against the weak position of the surviving spouse. A scheme that would deprive the children of all their rights as long as one of the parents is still alive is felt by many as going to far. A compromise arrangement, under which the survivor can continue to have disposal of the entire estate while the children will solely receive certain rights to it proved more attractive. The report of this study was published in 1978. Partly because of the results of this study the Bill was strongly amended. However, now it is 1983 and law of inheritance has not been changed yet. Now the revised edition of the Bill is strongly disputed by notaries.

Research into problems related with alimony after dissolution of marriage (C. Cozijn, C. van der Werff, 1981)

Background
During the late sixties the IWOG (Interdepartmental Working Party on Incomplete Families) published a report on the financial position of so-called incomplete families. These days they would be named one-parent-families to get rid of the connation that one-parent-families lack something or are not a real unity just because of the fact that one parent is missing: i.e. each family is complete, no matter what number and kind of persons it consists of. In this report it was mentioned that financial problems in one-parent families were mostly found amongst divorced women. So most of the report was devoted to ways of loosening the financial strains that these families suffer from. The report itself suffered from a lack of facts concerning the amount of alimony that divorced women were granted. During the early seventies, when divorce laws had been changed, the pressure to change alimony law too became stronger and stronger, especially with respect to duration of the duty to pay alimony.

A first question arrived at the RDC to answer the question what it might cost governments social security funds and taxes if alimony was to be deleted at all. So the search was now into the financial position of those who paid and those who received alimony. (For several reasons alimony for children was paid no attention.) The search showed that complete abolition of alimony after divorce would put considerable extra pressure on social security funds. This being so in a period of diminishing economical growth it became clear that other ways should be explored. A new working party was installed with the specific task to study the problem of imposing time limits to alimony duties, to develop several models in response of that question and to make an estimate of the consequences of each of these models.

During the proceedings of this working party it was understood that, if there was a proposal for the limitation of the duration of alimony duties to be made, one could not dispense with the attitudes of the population in these matters. So the RDC was asked to study the attitudes towards the limitation of maintenance, as well as to estimate the financial consequences of the various models for this limitation made by the above mentioned working party.

The results

In order to get answers to these questions a sample of the population, as well as a sample of ever-divorced people, were interviewed. They were to be asked whether to their opinions alimony was to be paid in four fictitious divorce cases. The cases differed from each other as to whether there were children or not, whether the wife had a job or professional training or not and whether the marriage had lasted a long time or just a few years. People were asked to tell, if alimony was to be paid in case, how long the payment should be made. The most important finding was that most of the respondents preferred some kind of temporary maintenance arrangement. In all fictitious cases the "no alimony" arrangement was most strongly opposed by more than half of the interviews. In these respects hardly any difference was seen between men and women, husbands and wives. Strikingly unexpected was the finding that the young (and unmarried) people (18-25 years of age) were so much in favour of everlasting alimonies. Divorced women preferred more often a permanent arrangement than divorced men. The latter were more in favour of temporary payments or no payments at all. Though the socio-demographic variables of sex, age, marital status, income bracket, degree of urbanisation, region and religious denomination seem to have some bearing on the subject, it turned out that they explain only a small proportion of the differences of opinion on maintenance payments. It was hypothesised that the attitude towards marriage, the traditional sex-role differentiation and the opinions on the women's lib movement would lead to an explanation that fits better. These attitudes have been observed by means of presenting sets of statements on these matters and asking the respondents to tell how strongly they agreed or disagreed with those statements. It happened that the correlations between these attitudes and the attitudes concerning the limitation of the duration of the duty to pay alimony turned out to be weak,though one could say that people who are more "modernist" on marriage were more in favour of relatively shorter alimony duties. This research was published in 1978 (financial consequences for government and social security that results from abolition of alimony), 1981 (Interimreport on the relation between opinions on the duration of alimony-duties and socio-demographic characteristics of the Dutch population), 1982 (as part of the report of the above mentioned working party "Limits on duration of alimony duties") and 1983 (Final report, concerning the relation between attitudes towards duration of alimony and marriage etc.).

Research into surnames: studies relating to articles 5 and 9 of part I of the Dutch civil code (M.W. Bol, A. Klijn, 1981)

Background
July 1978 the National Advisory Committee on Emancipation Affairs sent the Minister of Justice its recommendations on the matter of surnames in the Civil Code. These recommendations concentrated on two topics, first the names of married women, and second the surnames of children (legitimate or not).

Article 9 of book I of the Civil Code provides the married wives with the right to use their husbands names besides their own names or their husbands names followed by her maidennames, as happens to be customary. In day to day practice however, more and more married women encountered difficulties when using their maidennames. Article 5 states that the name of the legitimate child is its fathers'. This is objected because of the choice of the husbands name only is based on the out-of-date idea of the husband as head of the family. Besides that by this choice illegitimate children are recognizable just on their mother's name which is theirs too. The research had a twofold objective, first to gain an understanding of the historical development of Dutch custom and law regarding surnames and to survey systems elsewhere, and second to investigate the nature and extent of the objections of the naming system felt in present day society and any changes desired in the system. The former objective was to be reached in a study of literature, the latter by means of field surveys and analyses of invoked correspondence from those married women who used their won maiden names and not their husbands'.

The results

It was found that just an extremely small category of married women use their maiden name officially (some 1-2%). Their is cause to assume, however, that this number will increase considerably in the years to come. If they were to have the choice now, 27% of the married women under the age of 35 years would keep using their maiden name. It is quite a distinct category that uses the maiden name: young, well educated and just recently married and living in the large towns and cities. The most important reasons for not using their husbands name were "to behold one's own identity" and the feeling that men and women should have equal rights. The most important objection towards the present naming system is that there is a lack of choice. Among wives using their maiden name and among divorced women this concentrates on the fact that the legitimate born child cannot be given its mothers surname.

Names burned out to have two aspects in the day to day experience: first they can express a sense of belonging together and second they can stipulate one's own identity. These aspects are not mutually exclusive, it is more a matter of emphasis on the one or the other. People with more traditionalist attitudes towards marriage and sex-role differentiations placed the emphasis on the belonging together aspect, and the more modernist ones stressed on the own identity. This study was reported in 1982.

Research to come

At this moment there are two new research issues at the RDC in the field of family law. The first one concentrates on another consequence of divorce: custody and visitation rights for the non-custodial parent with the children. At first this study was to be focussed on the effects of the newly proposed Bill to amend law concerning these matters. But Parliamentary discussion on these Bill has stuck, and it is not even sure that it will reach the end, that is that the Bill will become law. In that case the research on custody and visitation-rights will have a severe change in focus. As long as this uncertainty continues it will not be possible to present more details of this study.

The second new research issue is not a search into family law itself. It has, however, such close connection with that matter that it would be ill advised not to mention it here. The project will focus on the role of lawyers in divorce and divorce-related proceedings. Not being able to proceed at court without legal representation by a lawyer it is not possible for divorcees not to attend with a lawyer. Lawyers, however, do not solely represent their clients in court proceedings, but will advise them on (socio)legal matters too. Besides that there is an counselling aspect in their activities. The study has been induced by a proposal for abolition of the obligatory legal representation. The purpose is to arrive at a solution where one doesn't throw out the baby (legal advise, counselling) with the bathwater (legal representation).

Conclusion

Most research at the RDC is focussed at issues that have a direct bearing on the policy of the Ministry of Justice, or for proposals to change law. This goes as well for the research into family law. So, all of the above-mentioned studies had their effects in the processes of policy making and preparing law amendments.
- The inheritance study took part in the process of opposing the amendments in such a way that the Bill, that was nicknamed "relief train" in order to get earlier at the desired destination, has been caught up by the one it was to relieve.
- The alimony studies played an important part in the discussion concerning the proposal for the amendment of the substantial divorce laws.
- The study on surnames has given rise to a new proposal to amend law on these issues.

So researchers on family law at the RDC play an important role in government policy making. This role, although satisfying, puts considerably stress on them. The main issue in this context is to get not too much mixed-up with the position of the policymakers and to stick to scientific standards only.

Bibliography: The sociology of law in the Dutch-speaking countries

M. GYSELS

Alphabetical order*

ANJOU, L.J.M. D', *Alternatieve sancties* [Alternative sanctions].
W.O.D.C., Den Haag, 1976.

ANJOU, L.J.M. D', *Invloed van belangen op wetgeving* [The effect of
interests on legislation]. E.U.R., Rotterdam, 1982.

ANJOU, L.J.M. D', G. de JONGE, J.J. van der KAADEN, *Effectiviteit
van sancties* [Effectiveness of sanctions]. W.O.D.C., Den Haag, 1975.

ANJOU, L.J.M. D', J.J. van der KAADEN, Wetgeving en sociale
wetenschappen *[Legislation and the social sciences]. Justitiële
verkenningen* No. 1 (1978), 4-26.

BAKKER-van der A.M. et al. Stagiaire-enquête *[Survey among apprentice-
Advocates]. Advokatenblad* (1970), 3-24.

BANDA, P.H., N.N.M. ROOS, Het gebruik van de huuradviescommissie
als conflictinstantie *[The use of the Rent Advisory Committee as
Conflict Regulating Authority]. Rechtssociologische Mededelingen* No.
10, Groningen.

BEEK, E.C. van de, G.B.M. ENGBERSEN, J.J. van der VEEN,
Participant observation in an advice bureaux, *N.N.R.* (1983) 2,
307-325.

BENDA-BECKMANN, K. von, F. STRIJBOSCH (red.), *Folk law and legal
pluralism in the Netherlands*. Foris Publications, Dordrecht, 1984.

BERCKMANS, P., C. de VOCHT, J. van HOUTTE, *Adoptie, een
rechtssociologische benadering* [Adoption, a socio-legal approach]. De
Sikkel/De Nederlandsche Boekhandel, Antwerpen/Amsterdam, 1981.

BERENDS, M., *Een tipje van de toga* [A corner of the toga]. Sociologisch

* Systemetical order: see p. 99.

Instituut, R.U.G., 1979.

BERENDS, M., E. HEKMAN, "Dokteren aan de omgang". De rol van huisartsen bij de totstandkoming van een bezoekregeling bij echtscheiding. [The role of general practitioners in the establishment of a visiting regulation after divorce]. *Rechtssociologische Mededelingen* No. 6, Groningen.

BERGHUIS, A.C., L.C.M. TIGGES, *Voorlopige hechtenis: toepassing, schorsing en zaken met lange duur* [Arrest: decisions to continue or to let go and cases of long duration]. W.O.D.C., Den Haag, 1981.

BERGHUIS-van der WIJK, I.J., Vermitteln oder Prozessieren? Faktoren die die Häufigkeit gütlicher Beilegung bei Rechtsanwälten beeinflussen *[Suing or mediating? Factors influencing the chances of a settlement by advocates] Blankenburg, Gottwald, Strempel,* Alternatieven in der Ziviljustiz [Alternatives in Civil Law]. *Bundesanzeige*, Köln, 1982.

BERGHUIS-van der WIJK, I.J., M.J.P. BRAND-KOOLEN, P. VINKE et al. *Houding ten aanzien van enkele aspecten van belastingheffing* [Attitudes concerning certain aspects of taxation]. Leiden, Rijksuniversiteit Leiden, afd. Rechtssociologie, 1970.

BERGSMA, R.L., *In verzekerde bewaring* [Arrest]. Boom, Meppel, 1977.

BERGSMA, R.L., P.J. VERBERNE, *Recht op en neer. Drie jaar experimentele ontwikkeling in de rechtshulp* [Justice up and down. Three years of experimental development in legal aid]. Het Juridisch Consultatiebureau, Amsterdam, 1974.

BLANKENBURG, E., *Innovations of the legal services*. Kronstein and Cambridge, Mass., 1980a.

BLANKENBURG, E., Mobilisierung von Recht [The mobilisation of justice]. *Zeitschrift für Rechtssoziologie*, 1 (1980b) 1.

BLANKENBURG, E., *Het idee van een maatschappij zonder recht* [The idea of a society without law]. Inaugurele Rede, Vrije Universiteit Amsterdam, 1982a.

BLANKENBURG, E., Legal insurance, litigant decisions and the rising caseload of courts. *Law and Society Review*, 16 (1982b) 4.

BLANKENBURG, E., The role of sociology of law in reforming procedural law: An annoted bibliographjy. *N.N.R.* (1983a) 2, 241-261.

BLANKENBURG, E., Bericht Niederlande [News of the Netherlands]. *Rechtssoziologie und Prozessrecht*. Berichte des 7. Internationalen Kongresses für Zivilprozessrecht in Würzburg, 1983b.

BLANKENBURG, E., Evaluation des ersten Jahres Beratungshilfe [Evaluation of the first year legal aid]. *Zeitschrift für Rechtspolitik*, 16 (1983c) 2.

BLANKENBURG, E., Evaluatie van de advies- en onderwijsfunctie van Rechtshulp – V.U. [Evaluation of the advice and teaching function of the legal clinic at the Free University of Amsterdam]. *Ars Aequi*, 1984.

BLANKENBURG, E., J. COOPER, A survey of legal aid literature in Europe. *Windsor Yearbook of Access to Justice* (1982) 2.

BLANKENBURG, E., J. FIEDLER, *Die Rechtsversicherungen und der steigende Geschäftsanfall der Gerichte* [Legal insurance and the rising caseloads of courts]. Mohr, Tübingen, 1981.

BLANKENBURG, E., U. REIFNER, *Rechtsberatung. Die soziale Definition von Rechtsproblemen* [Legal services. The social definition of legal problems]. Luchterhand, Neuwied, 1982.

BLANKENBURG, E., R. ROGOWSKI, Zur Theorie von Gerichtsverfahren [Towards a theory of court procedure]. *Zeitschrift für Rechtssoziologie*, 4 (1983) 2.

BLANKENBURG, E., D. STREMPEL, W. GOTTWALD (eds.), *Alternativen in der Ziviljustiz* [Alternatives in civil justice]. Bundesanzeigerverlag, Köln, 1982.

BLANKENBURG, E., H. TREIBER, V. BAUER, *Arbeitsplatz-Gericht, Modellversuch zur Humanisierung der Gerichtsorganisation Frankfurt* [Labour court, experiment for the humanisation of judicial organisation]. Campus, Frankfurt, 1983.

BLEGVAD, B.M., C. CAMPBELL, C.J.M. SCHUYT (ed.), *European Yearbook on law and sociology*. Martinus Nijhoff, The Hague, 1978.

BLOEMBERGEN, A.R., J.C. HERS-van HOVE, P. VINKE et al. *Duizend botsingen; een kwantitatieve analyse van de civiele rechtbankvonnisen in verkeerszaken* [Thousand crashes; a quantitative analysis of civil court verdicts in traffic cases]. Kluwer, Deventer, 1972.

BLOEMBERGEN, A.R., P.J.M. van WERSCH, *Verkeersslachtoffers en hun schade* [Traffic victims and their damage] . Kluwer, Deventer, 1973.

BOEKMAN, S., *Verslag van de studiekommissie rechtsbijstand aan on- en minvermogenden* [Report on the Bar-commission of legal aid for the poor]. Nederlandse Orde van Advocaten, Den Haag, 1972 en 1977.

BOL, M.W., A. KLIJN, *Achternamen; onderzoek in verband met de artikelen 5 en 9 van het Burgerlijk Wetboek* [Surnames; studies relating to articles 5 and 9 of the Code Civil]. Staatsuitgeverij, Den Haag, 1981.

BORGHT, G. van der, Rapport: meningen van de bevolking over de verdeling van nalatenschappen onder het ab intestaat erfrecht [Public opinions concerning the distribution of inheritances under the law of succession "ab intestato"]. *Nederlands Juristenblad* (1978), 745-750.

BOS, A.M., Holland and the computerization of the law. *Law and Computer Technology*, May/June 1970a, 119-121.

BOS, A.M., Jurimetrie [Jurimetrics]. Van Houtte, J., C.M.J. Schuyt et al. *Rechtssociologie en jurimetrie* [Sociology of law and jurimetrics]. Kluwer, Deventer, 1970b, 97-112.

BOS, A.M., De plaats van de juridische informatica in de rechtscultuur [The place of legal information retrieval in legal culture]. de Graaf, F. (red.), *Computer en Recht* [Computer and the Law]. Deventer, 1972, 55-66.

BOS, A.M., Versluierd vertrouwen [Veiled confidence]. *Bestuurswetenschappen* (July, 1975a), 282-289.

BOS, A.M., Over rechtsvinding en sociologie [On adjudication and sociology], *'t Exempel dwinght*, Feestbundel voor Prof. I. Kisch. Tjeenk Willink, Zwolle, 1975b, 27-36.

BOS, A.M., *De voorgeschiedenis der grondrechten* [On the history of human rights]. Deventer, 1976a.

BOS, A.M., Wetgeven in een technotronische samenleving [Legislation in a technotronic society]. *Bestuurswetenschappen* (May/June, 1976b), 182-192.

BOS, A.M., Logica als hulpmiddel van de rechtswetenschap [Logic as a resource for legal science]. *Kennis en Methode* (178) 2, 140-154.

BOS, A.M., Rechtswetenschap in bedrijf [Legal science in action]. *Intermediair*, 16 (1980) 4, 1, 3, 5, 7, 31.

BOS, A.M., Recht [Law and Legal Science]. Bergman, H.H.J. (red.), *Zo ver is de wetenschap* [The progress of science]. Utrecht, 1982, 169-175.

BRAAM, A. van, H.G. SURIE, *Toestand en toekomst van de Nederlandse Balie, een organisatie-verkenning* [Present and future of the Dutch Bar, an organisation- exploration]. Rotterdam, May 1972.

BREDA, J. Legal aid in Belgium. *N.N.R.* (1983) 2, 360-361.

BREDA, J., A. STEVENS, J. van HOUTTE, *Rechtshulp aan marginalen* [Legal aid to marginals], Nationaal Onderzoeksprogramma in de Sociale Wetenschappen, Diensten van de Eerste Minister,

Programmatie van het Wetenschapsbeleid. Brussel, 1981a.

BREDA, J., A. STEVENS, J. van HOUTTE, *Algemene sociale rechtshulp: de Openbare Centra voor Maatschappelijk Welzijn* [General socio-legal aid: The Public Assistance Agencies], Nationaal Onderzoeksprogramma in de Sociale Wetenschappen, Diensten van de Eerste Minister, Programmatie van het Wetenschapsbeleid. Brussel, 1981b.

BREDA, J., A. STEVENS, J. van HOUTTE, *Algemene sociale rechtshulp: de Balie* [General social legal aid: The Bar], Nationaal Onderzoeksprogramma in de Sociale Wetenschappen, Diensten van de Eerste Minister, Programmatie van het Wetenschapsbeleid. Brussel, 1981c.

BREDA, J., A. STEVENS, J. van HOUTTE, *Algemene sociale rechtshulp: de Wetswinkels* [General social legal aid: The Law Shops], Nationaal Onderzoeksprogramma in de Sociale Wetenschappen, Diensten van de Eerste Minister, Programmatie van het Wetenschapsbeleid. Brussel, 1981d.

BREDA, J., A. STEVENS, J. van HOUTTE, *Rechtshulp aan marginalen. Syntheserapport* [Legal aid to marginals. Synthetic report], Nationaal Onderzoeksprogramma in de Sociale Wetenschappen, Diensten van de Eerste Minister, Programmatie van het Wetenschapsbeleid. Brussel, 1981e.

BROEKMAN, J.M., A.C. 't HART, *Norm changing behaviour and judicial policy*. Acco, Leuven, 1980.

BRUINSMA, F., Het recht van de zwakste [The rights of the weakest]. *De Gids* (1978), 101-108.

BRUINSMA, F., Balans van de rechtssociologie over de jaren '70 [A review of sociology of law in the seventies]. *Nederlands Juristenblad*, 55 (1980) 20, 437-449.

BRUINSMA, F., Hollandse (en Vlaamse) Nieuwe in de rechtssociologie [Dutch and Flemish novelties in sociology of law]. *Nederlands Juristenblad* (1983a) 10, 307-311.

BRUINSMA, F., Het recht op verzet [The right to oppose]. Heringa, A.W., R.E. de Winter, J.W. Witteveen (red.), *Staatkundige Pamfletten* [Political pamphlets] No. 1. Leiden, 1983b.

BUIKHUIZEN, W., J.J.M. van DIJCK, *Official police reporting of criminal offences*. W.O.D.C., Den Haag, 1975.

72

CLAESSENS, T.M.A., M.I. 't HOOFT, J.I.M. JACOPS et al., De balie, een leemte in de rechtshulp? [The Bar, a gap in legal aid?]. *Ars Aequi*, 19 (1970) 6, 223-314.

COZIJN, C., Privacy en persoonsregistratie [Privacy and personal registrations]. *Justitiële verkenningen* No. 5 (1977).

COZIJN, C., *Meningen van de bevolking over de verdeling van nalatenschappen onder het ab intestaat erfrecht* [Public opinion on the distribution of estates under the law of intestacy]. W.O.D.C., Den Haag, 1978a.

COZIJN, C., *De financiële consequenties voor de overheid van een wettelijke limitering van de duur van de onderhoudsplicht van ex-echtgenoten jegens elkaar* [Financial consequences of the legal limitations of the duration of alimony duty between ex-spouses for the government]. W.O.D.C., Den Haag, 1978b.

COZIJN, C., Echtscheiding: een bron van problemen [Divorce: A source of problems]. *Justitiële verkenningen* No. 5 (1981).

COZIJN, C., *Echtscheiding, de opvattingen over alimentatie na echtscheiding en de wetgeving in Nederland.* Voordracht op de Nederlands-Belgische Studiedag "Gevolgen van echtscheiding", van de Nederlandse Vereniging voor Demografie [Divorce, the public opinion concerning alimony after divorce and legislation in the Netherlands. Lecture given at the Dutch-Belgian Symposium on "Consequences of divorce" of the Dutch Society for Demography]. Tilburg, 1982.

COZIJN, C., Research in the sociology of law at the Research and Documentation Center of the Ministry of Justice in the Netherlands. *N.N.R.* (1983) 2, 299-306.

COZIJN, C., C. van der WERFF, *Meningen van de Nederlandse bevolking over alimentatie na echtscheiding* [Public opinions in the Netherlands on alimony following divorce]. Staatsuitgeverij, Den Haag, 1981.

CROMBAG, H.F.M., J.L. de WIJKER SLOOTH, M.J. COHEN, *Een theorie over rechterlijke belissingen* [A theory of judicial decision-making]. Tjeenk Willink, Groningen, 1977.

DASSEN, K., M. van der HEYDEN (red.), *The advocate: The position of the advocate in the Judicial Code of Law.* Universitaire Kring voor Rechtstheorie. Kluwer, Antwerpen, 1978.

DOORN, J.A.A. van, C.J.M. SCHUYT (ed.), *De stagnerende verzorgingsstaat* [The stagnant welfare state]. Boom, Meppel, 1978.

DUINTJER-KLEIN, M.R., Rechtshulp [Legal aid]. *Justitiële verkenningen*, Documentatieblad van het Ministerie van Justitie (1976) 4, 146-161.

DUYNE, P.C. van, *Beslissen in eenvoud* [Decisionmaking in singular]. Arnhem, 1983.

FRANKEN, H., *Vervolgingsbeleid – een juridimetrisch onderzoek betreffende het vervolgingsbeleid van het Openbaar Ministerie inzake art. 26 van de Wegenverkeerswet* [Prosecution policy – a juridimetric analysis of prosecutors decisions with respect to drunk driving]. Diss. Amsterdam, 1973; Garda Quint, Arnhem, 1973.

FRID, A., et al. Rechtshulp [Legal aid]. *Justitiële verkenningen*, Documentatieblad van het Ministerie van Justitie (1976) 4, 145-192.

FRID, A., *Panklaar voor de zitting – de praktijk van het strafproces rondom de rechter-commissaris* [Done with before trial – The reality of penal process before the investigation-judge]. Gouda Quint, Arnhem, 1982.

GEERTS, P., De rechtshulp in België [Legal aid in Belgium]. *Recht en Kritiek* (1977) 4, 413-428.

GILS, A.J., M.G. van WESTEROP, Rechtsbijstand onbereikbaar? Een onderzoek onder kliënten van de Wetswinkel te Rotterdam [Unreachable legal aid? A survey among the clients of a law shop in Rotterdam]. *Mededelingen van het Juridisch Instituut van de Nederlandse Economische Hogeschool* No. 1 (1972).

GLASTRA van LOON, J.F., De ijdelheid van beslisssingen [The vanity of decisions]. *Handelingen van de Nederlandse Vereniging van Bestuursrecht*, 1984.

GOEDMAKERS, S., Bibliografie van sociaal-wetenschappelijk werk inzake het functioneren van schaderegelingen en aansprakelijkheidsnormen, in het bijzonder bij verkeers- en andere ongevallen [Socio-scientific bibliography concerning the functioning of damage regulations and responsibility norms, especially in traffic and other accidents]. *Rapporten Rechtssociologie*. Juridische Faculteit, Universiteit van Amsterdam, Amsterdam, 1980.

GOOSSENS, P., J. JASPERS, M. de VOS, "Tussen nulde- en tweede lijn". Een onderzoek naar het functioneren van de Buro's voor Rechtshulp in Groningen en Drente [A research on the functioning of the legal aid offices of Groningen and Drente]. *Rechtssociologische Mededelingen* No. 8, Groningen.

GRAS, F.A.J. *Standaardkontrakten; een rechtssociologische analyse* [Standard contracts; an analysis from the point of view of sociology of law]. Deventer, 1979.

GRAS, F.A.J., Bijlagen, behorend bij F.A.J. Gras, *Standaardkontrakten; een rechtssociologische analyse* [Appendix to F.A.J. Gras, Standard contracts; an analysis from the point of view of sociology of law]. Amsterdam, 1980.

GRAS, F.A.J., Deponering van algemene voorwaarden; enige rechtssociologische kanttekeningen [Registration of general conditions; some comments from the side of the sociology of law]. *W.P.N.R.*, 112 (1982a) 5564 en 5565, 305-311 en 320-3.

GRAS, F.A.J., Standaard contracten: contracten nieuwe stijl [Standard contracts: "New Style"-contracts]. Hoekema, A.J., J. van Houtte (red.), *De rechtssociologische werkkamer* [Work in progress in sociology of law]. Van Loghum Slaterus, Deventer, 1982b, 155-178.

GRAS, F.A.J., Het standaardkontrakt en de verhouding recht/maatschappij [The standard contract and the relation between law and society]. *R.M. Themis* (1983a) 1, 6-30.

GRAS, F.A.J., *Standaardkontrakten; Verslag van het onderzoek "Standaardkontrakten", deel II, toetsingsonderzoek, beschrijvend onderzoek en analyse van standaardkontrakten* [Standard contracts; Report of the research project "Standard contracts", part II, testing, description and analysis]. Amsterdam, 1983b.

GRIFFITHS, J., The distribution of legal services in the Netherlands (review essay on C. Schuyt et al., De weg naar het recht, 1976). *British Journal of Law and Society* (1977) 4, 260.

GRIFFITHS, J., Enkele onderscheidingen die aan alle zinvolle vraagstellingen ten aanzien van recht voorafgaan [Some distinctions preceding every meaningful legal questioning]. *Ars Aequi* (1978a) 28, 839.

GRIFFITHS, J., Some aspects of the distribution of grading appeals in three Dutch law faculties. *N.Y. University Review of Law and Social Change*, 7 (1978b), 1-13.

GRIFFITHS, J., Is law important? *N.Y. University Law Review*, 54 (1979 a), 339-374.

GRIFFITHS, J., Legal reasoning from the external and the internal perspectives: The legal philosophy of R. Dworkin. *Nederlands*

Juristenblad (24.3.1979), 237-247; also: *N.Y. University Law Review*, 53 (1979b), 1124-1149.

GRIFFITHS, J., A comment on research into "legal needs". Blankenburg, E. (ed.), *Innovations in the Legal Services*. Oelgeschlager, Gun and Haen, Cambridge, Mass., 1980.

GRIFFITHS, J., Review of S. Burman and B. Hariel-Bond. The imposition of Law (1979). *Modern Law Review*, 44 (1981), 352.

GRIFFITHS, J., Recht en Ontwikkeling [Justice and development]. *Recht en Kritiek* (1983a), 175-191.

GRIFFITHS, J., The general theory of litigation – a first step. *Zeitschrift für Rechtssoziologie*, 5 (1983b), 145-201.

GRIFFITHS, J., Antropology of law in the Netherlands in the 1970s. *N.N.R.*, 4 (1983c),, 143-240.

GRIFFITHS, J., Research in progress: The processes by which divorcing parents arrange the future of their children; in particular visitations. *N.N.R.* (1983d) 2, 362-391.

GRIFFITHS, J., The division of labor and social control. Forthcoming in: Black, D. (ed.), *Toward a general theory of social control*. Academic Press, New York, 1984a.

GRIFFITHS, J., Heeft de rechtssociologie een toegevoegde waarde? Reflecties naar aanleiding van een oratie van K. Schuyt). [Has sociology of law an added value ? Reflections on an oration by K. Schuyt]. *Mens en Maatschappij* (1984b) 59, 82-97; a more extensive version appears in: *N.N.R.* (1984) 1, 99-123.

GRIFFITHS, J., Four laws of interaction in circumstances of legal pluralism: Paper delivered at the conference of the Commission on Folk Law and Legal Pluralism, Bellagio, September 1981; forthcoming in: Allat, A., G. Woodman (eds.), *People's law and state law: The Bellagio papers*. Foris publications, Dordrecht.

GROENENDAEL, A.J.M. van, *Meesters in de bestuur* [Lawyers in the public administration; a normative analysis of the impact of a juridical background on administrative decisionmaking]. Tjeenk Willink, Zwolle, 1973.

GROENENDAEL, A.J.M. van, Legalizing illegal aliens: A case study in regulatory justice. *N.N.R.* (1983) 2, 347-360.

GROENENDAEL, A.J.M. van, A. van der VAART, *Buitenlanders en Buro's voor Rechtshulp* [Aliens and the legal aid services; an analysis of registred visitors and the problems they address to the legal aid services]. Instituut voor Rechtssociologie, Nijmegen, 1983.

GROENENDAEL, A.J.M. van, et al. (red.), De leemte bij de balie opgevuld? [Legal aid by non legal aid services, fiscal institutions, lailiffs, etc.]. *J.S.V.U.-bulletin* No. 1, Utrecht, 1971.

GROENENDIJK, C.A., Van gunst tot recht: het Nederlandse paspoortrecht [From favour to right: The Dutch law on passports]. *Intermediair* (1973a) 22 en 38.

GROENENDIJK, C.A., Rechts(on)zekerheid in het vreemdelingenrecht, [(Un)security in the immigration legislation]. *Intermediair* (1973b) 40.

GROENENDIJK, C.A., Juss-buss: alternatieve en aktieve rechtshulp [Juss-buss: Alternative and active legal assistance]. *Legal aid − a proof of incapacity*. Amsterdam, 1974, 72-84.

GROENENDIJK, C.A., Class-action, een voorbeeld van groepsactie voor de rechter [Class-action: an example of group action in court]. *Nederlands Juristenblad* (1975a), 233-252.

GROENENDIJK, C.A., De rechterlijke macht in Nederland: tussen balie en bureaucratie [The judicature in the Netherlands: Between bar and bureaucracy]. *Beleid en Maatschappij* (1975b), 151-165.

GROENENDIJK, C.A., Legal aid to immigrants in the Netherlands: How layers discovered a new branch of law and provided representation to a new class of clients. *Flere emner fra fremmdrelten*. Institutt for offentlig ret, Oslo, 1978.

GROENENDIJK, C.A., Van gastarbeider tot medeburger [From guestworker to fellow citizen]. *Beleid en Maatschappij* (1979), 52-63.

GROENENDIJK, C.A., The working group on legal aid for immigrants: A public interest law organisation in the Netherlands. *Delivery of Legal Services*. Cambridge, Mass., 1981a.

GROENENDIJK, C.A., *Bundeling van belangen, bij de burgerlijke rechter [Representing collective interests in civil courts]*. Dissertation Zwolle, 1981b.

GROENENDIJK, C.A., Minderhedenbeleid in een onwillig immigratieland [Policy concerning etnic minorities in an recalcitrant immigration-country]. *Ars Aequi* (1981c), 531-546.

GROENENDIJK, C.A., Die Wahrnehmung gebündelter Interessen im Zivilprozess [The representation of collective interests in civil litigation]. *Zeitschrift für Rechtssoziologie* (1982a), 240-271.

GROENENDIJK, C.A., Juridische gevolgen van sluikarbeid onder immigrantenarbeiders [Legal consequences of illegal employment of immigrant workers]. *Sociaal Maandblad Arbeid* (1982b), 828-836.

GROENENDIJK, C.A., Recht en rassendiscriminatie: een januskop met legel handen? [Law and racial discrimination: A Janus-face with empty hands?]. *Congress on Law and Race Relations*. Arnhem, 1983a, 11-21.

GROENENDIJK, C.A., (De)regulering van de rechtshulp [(De)regulating legal aid]. *Advocatenblad* (1983b), 277-279.

GROENENDIJK, C.A., Recht tegen rassendiscriminatie op de arbeidsmarkt [Legal action against racial discrimination in employment]. *Sociaal Maandblad Arbeid* (1983c), 660-672.

GROENENDIJK, C.A., Trouwbeperkingen voor tweede generatie immigranten. Minderhedenbeleid en mensenrechten dicht bij huis [Restricting family reunion for second generation immigrants: minorities policy and human rights at home]. *Nederlands Juristenblad* (1983d), 1311-1318.

GROENENDIJK, C.A., C.J.M. SCHUYT, B.P. SLOOT, Rechtsprobleme oder private Schwierigkeiten. Die Jurisprudenznahme von Rechtshilfe in den Niederlanden [Legal problems or private troubles]. *Rechtsbedürfnis und Rechtshilfe, empirische Ansätze im internationalen Vergleich*. Westdeutscher Verlag, Wiesbaden, 1975, 109-138.

GROENENDIJK, C.A. C.J.M. SCHUYT, B.P. SLOOT, Dilemma's in de juridische hulpverlening [Dilemmas of legal assistance]. *Jura Falconis* (1976), 426-454.

GROENENDIJK, C.A., A.H.J. SWART, Het verblijf en de vestiging van Surinamers in Nederland [The admission and residence of Surinamese immigrants in the Netherlands] *Nederlands Juristenblad* (1975), 941-950.

GROENENDIJK, C.A., A.H.J. SWART, Aliens, human rights and the right to vote in municipal elections in the Netherlands. *Etudes migrations* No. 49, Rome, 1978.

GROENENDIJK, C.A., T. van GROENENDAEL, T. HAVINGA et al., De sociale betekenis van de afwijzende rechtspositie [The social meaning of the special legal status of immigrants]. *N.N.R.* (1982) 2, 73-88.

GYSELS, M., J. van HOUTTE, M. VOGELS, *Het echtpaar op weg naar*

gelijkheid? Een confrontatie van huwelijkswetgeving en gezinsrealiteit
[Husband and wife on their way to equality? A confrontation of
marriage legislation and family reality]. De Nederlandsche
Boekhandel, Antwerpen, 1984.

GYSELS, M., M. VOGELS, Belgian husbands and wives: equal in
patrimonial matters? *International Journal of Sociology of Law* (1982)
10, 205-216.

HANNEMA, E., Rechtshulp of zelfhulp? Onderzoek van de spreekuren van
Rechtshulp, V.U. [Legal aid or self-help? Research on the office-hours
of the V.U.-Legal Aid Office] *Rechtshulp*, 1983.

HAVINGA, T., Van hun kant bekeken; *Turkse en Surinaamse kranten over
rechtspositie en problemen van immigranten* [Turkish and Surinam
newspapers on legal position and problems of immigrants]. Katholieke
Universiteit, Faculteit der Rechtsgeleerdheid, Nijmegen, 1983.

HES, J., *Tussen wal en schip – tussen recht en hulpverlening. Een
empirisch-theoretische verkenning in de eerste lijns(rechts)hulp*
[Between law and assistance. An empirical-theoretical exploration of
first line (legal) aid]. Rotterdam, 1982.

HES, J., Terug naar een leemte in de rechtshulp [Back to a gap in legal aid].
Wiebrens, C. (red.), *Geen man overboord* [No one overboard]. De
Horstink, Amersfoort, 1983, 63-77.

HEUVEL, J. van den, Rechtsbijstandsverzekering [Legal aid insurance].
Rechtskundig Weekblad, 37 (1974) 35, 1934-1952.

HOEFNAGELS, G.P., *Rituelen der terechtzitting* [Rituals in Court].
Kluwer, Deventer, 1970.

HOEFNAGELS, G.P., *Een eenvoudige strafzitting. Een onderzoek naar de
doelstellingen, verwachtingen en uitkomsten van de methode van
strafrechtspraak in minder grote zaken* [Every-day penal court:
Research on goals, expectations and results of judicial decisions on
petty crime]. Samson, Alphen a.d. Rijn, 1980.

HOEKEMA, A.J., Rechtssociologie: zegen of ramp voor het recht [Legal
sociology: Heaven or hell for the law?]. *Proces*, 2 (1970a) 10,336-344.

HOEKEMA, A.J., Het kwaad der rechtssociologie [The evil side of
sociology of law]. *Trias*, 3 (1970b) 4, 67-84.

HOEKEMA, A.J., *Vertrouwen in de justitie. Resultaten van een
vergelijkend onderzoek [Confidence in justice: A comparative study]*.
Samson, Alphen a.d. Rijn, 1971.

HOEKEMA, A.J., Sociale wetenschap en wetgeving [The social sciences and the process of legislation]. Hoekema, A.J., C.J.A. Crasborn, *Social wetenschappen en wetgeving* [The social sciences and legislation]. Kluwer, Deventer, 1973, 4-53.

HOEKEMA, A.J., *Vertrouwen in de wetenschap* [Confidence in science]. Vrije Universiteit, Amsterdam, 1974.

HOEKEMA, A.J., Vertrouwen in recht en wet onder havenarbeiders [Confidence in justice and the law among port workers]. *Sociologica Neerlandica*, 11 (1975a) 2, 128-143.

HOEKEMA, A.J., Overmacht van maatschappelijke instellingen: recht of onrecht? [Power of social institutions: Legitimate or illegitimate?]. *Maandblad voor Geestelijke Volksgezondheid*, 30 (1975b) 1, 3-15.

HOEKEMA, A.J., *Openbaar bestuur en burger, voor zover zij elkaar uitsluitende tegendelen zijn geworden* [Public administration and the citizen as opponents]. Preadvies Calvinistische Juristen-Vereniging, Amsterdam, 1975c.

HOEKEMA, A.J., Book review of K. Schuyt "Law Order and Civil Disobedience", Rotterdam, 1975. *The Netherlands' Journal of Sociology*, 12 (1976a), 165-171.

HOEKEMA, A.J., De evoluerende eigendom [Property in evolution]. *Oosthoek's Encyclopedie*, 7e druk, also: *Intermediair*, 12 (1976b) 40, 53-55.

HOEKEMA, A.J., Klasse-justitie; een verwijzing naar enige literatuur [Class justice; some literature]. *Justitiële Verkenningen* (1976c) 10, 498-502, also *Oosthoek's Encyclopedie*, 7de druk.

HOEKEMA, A.J., Opsporings- en vervolgingsrichtlijnen, een rechtssociologisch onderzoek [Guidelines for prosecutorial decision making]. *Delikt en delinkwent* (1978a) 8, 443-488.

HOEKEMA, A.J., *Oriëntatie in de rechtssociologie* [Introductory remarks regarding sociology of law]. Amsterdam, 1978b.

HOEKEMA, A.J., *De uitgespeelde gemeenteraad. Beschrijving van de invloedsverdeling bij een rooilijnbesluit in een grote gemeente* [The city council down and out. Description of the contribution of influence in a case of urban planning in a big community]. Kluwer, Deventer, 1978c.

HOEKEMA, A.J., Recht in de rechtssociologie [The concept of law in legal sociology]. *Ars Aequi*, 28 (1979) 11, 852-870.

HOEKEMA, A.J., Rechtssociologische aantekeningen bij het schadevergoedingsrecht [Notes from a legal sociologist on the legal rules providing compensation and support for injury and damage]. *Nederlands Juristenblad*, 55 (1980a) 38, 977-1000; also: Verburgh, M.J.P. et al., *Schade lijden en schade dragen* [To suffer damage and to carry the consequences]. Zwolle, 1980a, 175-230.

HOEKEMA, A.J., Tegen evaluatieonderzoek [Against evaluation research]. *N.N.R.* (1980b) 1, 30-34.

HOEKEMA, A.J., Rationalisering van strafvorming [Rationalisation of the administration of criminal justice]. *Ad personam, opstellen aangeboden aan Ch.J. Enschedé* [Essays in honor of Ch.J. Enschedé]. Zwolle, 1981.

HOEKEMA, A.J., Dialoog als een centraal begrip in een normatieve (rechts)sociologie [Dialogue as a central concept in a normative sociology (of law)]. *N.N.R.* (1982) 2, 24-25.

HOEKEMA, A.J., E.A. HUPPES, Hedendaagse vraagstukken met betrekking tot de vormgeving van het ideaal van de rechtsstaat [Actual problems regarding the institutionalization of the ideal of the rule of law]. *Winkler Prins Encyclopedisch Jaarboek 1978*, 273-275.

HOEKEMA, A.J., J. van HOUTTE, *De rechtssociologische werkkamer* [Work in progress in sociology of law]. Van Loghum Slaterus, Deventer, 1982.

HOOFTMAN, J.C., *De advocaat en de rechtshulp* [The advocate and legal aid]. Tjeenk Willink, Zwolle,1 1976.

HOUTAPPEL, J.G., Access to justice in Holland. *Access to justice* Vol. I. Alphen a.d. Rijn, 1978, 579-594.

HOEVELS, B.W.M., G. KRIJNEN, *Functies van juristen. Een onderzoek naar de werkkringen van juristen die in de periode van september 1947 tot september 1972 zijn afgestudeerd* [The employment of lawyers. A research on the field of activity of lawyers who graduated from 1947 to 1972]. Instituut voor Toegepaste Sociologie, Nijmegen, 1974.

HOUTTE, J. van, Perspectieven van de rechtssociologie [The perspectives of sociology of law] Van Houtte, J., C.M.J. Schuyt et al., *Rechtssociologie en jurimetrie* [Sociology of law and jurimetrics]. Kluwer, Deventer, 1970a, 57-71).

HOUTTE, J. van, Les travaux du Centre de Recherches Economiques et Sociales – Facultés Universitaires Saint-Ignace à Anvers [The publications of the Centre of Economical and Social Research –

UFSIA, Antwerp]. *Actes du Colloque International de Sociologie du Droit et de la Justice.* Review de l'Institut de Sociologie (1970b) 2, 335-344.

HOUTTE, J. van, Socialization of the law. *Sociological Contributions from Flanders* 1969-1970. Antwerpen, 1971, 100-111.

HOUTTE, J. van, Rechtsbewustzijn, een rechtstheoretisch begrip, publieke opinie, een sociologisch begrip [Legal consciousness, a legal theoretical concept, Public opinion, a sociological concept]. *Recht in Beweging,* opstellen aangeboden aan Prof. mr. ridder R. Victor. Deurne/Antwerpen, 1973, 1241-1250.

HOUTTE, J. van, De plaats van de jurist in de komende samenleving [The position of lawyers in future society]. *Rechtskundig Weekblad,* 37 (1974) 41, 2352-2360.

HOUTTE, J. van, Het probleem van het onderwijs in de rechtssociologie in België [The problem of the socio-legal education in Belgium]. *Actori Incumbit Probatio.* Marten Kluwer's, Antwerpen – Amsterdam, 1975, 203-211.

HOUTTE, J. van, Familiesolidariteit versus gemeenschapssolidariteit [From family solidarity to community solidarity]. *Tijdschrift voor Sociaal Welzijn en Maatschappelijk Werk,* 4 (1977) 6, 194-199.

HOUTTE, J. van, Het huwelijk in rechtssociologisch perspectief [Marriage in a socio-legal perspective]. *Rechtskundig Weekblad,* 44 (1980) 5, 295-309.

HOUTTE, J. van, Gezinswerkelijkheid en recht. Een problematische verhouding [Family reality and justice. A problematical relationship]. Hoekema, A.J., J. van Houtte (red.), *De rechtssociologische werkkamer* [Work in progress in sociology of law]. Van Loghum Slaterus, Deventer, 1982a, 178-208.

HOUTTE, J. van, Adoption et protection de la jeunesse [Adoption and youth protection]. *Recherches Sociologiques.* Université Catholique de Louvain (1982b) 3, 285-309.

HOUTTE, J. van, Der Beitrag der Rechtssoziologie zur Reform des Prozessrecht in Belgien [The contribution of sociology of law to the judicial law reform in Belgium]. Roth, G.H. (herausgeber), *Rechtssoziologie und Prozessrecht* [Sociology of law and judicial law]. Orac, Wien, 1983a, 1-14.

HOUTTE, J. van, De mogelijke bijdrage van de rechtssociologie tot de hervorming van het gerechtelijk recht [A feasible contribution of sociology of law to the judicial law reform]. *Rechtskundig Weekblad*, 46 (1983b) 34, 2231-2242.

HOUTTE, J. van, A socio-legal approach of the problems of Administration of Justice in Belgium. *Effectiveness of judicial protection on constitutional order, Belgian report at the II International Congress of Procedural Law*. Kluwer, Deventer, 1983c, 1-13.

HOUTTE, J. van, Inaction of law: The Belgian adoption law. *N.N.R.* (1983d) 2, 296-298.

HOUTTE, J. van, M. BAX, La famigla et l'evoluzione del diritto in Belgio [Family and judicial evolution in Belgium]. Pocar, V., P. Ronfani, *Famigla, diritto, mutamento social in Europe*. Edizioni di Comunita, Milano, 1979, 47-63.

HOUTTE, J. van, J. BREDA, *Behoeftige bejaarden en onderhoudsplichtige kinderen. Een rechtssociologisch onderzoek in Commissie van Openbare Onderstand en Vredegerecht* [Elderly persons in need and children liable for their maintenance. A sociological survey of law practices in Public Assistance Agencies and Justice of the Peace Courts]. Van Loghum Slaterus, Deventer, 1976.

HOUTTE, J. van, J. BREDA, Maintenance between aged persons and their adult children. Family and state as agencies in the solution of poverty. *Law and Society Review*, 12 (1978) 4, 645-664.

HOUTTE, J. van, I. CALLENS, *Acceptance of fiscal legal norms in sociology of law and legal sciences*. Proceedings of a conference on the sociology of law, Balatonszéplak, Hungary, September 21-25, 1976. Institute of Sociology, Hungarian Academy of Sciences, Budapest, 1977, 237-247.

HOUTTE, J. van, I. CALLENS, R. LAFAILLE et al., *Aanvaarding van de rechtsnorm. Houdingen en opinies t.a.v. fiskaliteit en regels in de sociale biosfeer* [The acceptance of legal rules, opinions and attitudes towards fiscal matters and the ethical bio-sphere]. De Nederlandsche Boekhandel, Antwerpen, 1973.

HOUTTE, J. van, C. de VOCHT, Rechtssociologische analyse van de onderhoudsplicht tussen echtgenoten [A socio-legal analysis of alimony duty between spouses]. *Onderhoudsgeld*, juridische uitgaven, Universiteit Antwerpen, Departement Rechten. Ced-Samson, Brussel,

1978, 259-261.

HOUTTE, J. van, C. de VOCHT, The obligation to provide maintenance between divorced husband and wife. A social problem? *Law and Society Review*, 16 (1981-1982) 2, 501-514.

HOUTTE, J. van, G. DIERICKX, De rechtssociologie: haar ambities en beperkingen [Sociology of law: Its ambitions and limitations]. *Tijdschrift voor Privaatrecht* (1970) 4, 419-442.

HOUTTE, J. van, G. DIERICKX, La sociologie du droit, une science globalisante? [Sociology of law, a generalizing science?]. *Revue de l'Institut de Sociologie.* Université Libre de Bruxelles (1971) 4, 615-638.

HOUTTE, J. van, E. LANGERWERF, Juristen. Enkele basisstatistieken [Lawyers. Some basic statistics]. *Tijdschrift voor Privaatrecht*, 13 (1976) 1, 1-40.

HOUTTE, J. van, E. LANGERWERF, Activiteiten van hoven en rechtbanken. Enige sociografische gegevens [The activities of the courts. Some sociographical data]. *Tijdschrif voor Privaatrecht*, 14 (1977a) 1, 1-56.

HOUTTE, J. van, E. LANGERWERF, *Sociographical data on the judicial system. Lawyers-activities of courts and tribunals.* Kluwer, Antwerpen, 1977b.

HOUTTE, J. van, E. LANGERWERF, Recente trends in de evolutie van de activiteiten van de burgerlijke rechtbanken 1969-1972 [Recent trends in the evolution of the activities of the civil courts from 1969 till 1972]. *Rechtskundig Weekblad* (1977-1978), 1601-1606.

HOUTTE, J. van, E. LANGERWERF, Trends in de evolutie van de activiteit van de burgerlijke rechtbanken [Trends in the evolution of the activity of civil courts from 1972 till 1977]. *Rechtskundig Weekblad* (1978-1979), 707-712.

HOUTTE, J. van, E. LANGERWERF, De fiscale rechtspraak van het Hof van Beroep te Antwerpen. Elementen van een rechtssociologische analyse [The administration of justice by the Court of Appeal of Antwerp in fiscal matters. Elements of a socio-legal analysis]. *Rechtskundig Weekblad* (1979-1980), 1265-1290.

HOUTTE, J. van, E. LANGERWERF, La justice en matière fiscale: le cas de la Court d'Appel d'Anvers [Justice in fiscal affairs: The Court of Appeal of Antwerp]. *Sociologie du Travail, Sociologie et Justice* (1981) 1, 50-56.

HOUTTE, J. van, E. LANGERWERF, The administration of justice by the fiscal affairs chamber of the Court of Appeal of Antwerp. Cain, M., K. Kulcsar (edit.), *Disputes and the law*. Akademiai Kiado, Budapest, 1983, 135-143.

HOUTTE, J. van, F. REYNTJENS, A. BASOMINGERA, Litiges et besoins juridiques au Rwanda [Lawsuits and juridical needs in Rwanda]. *Revue Juridique du Rwanda* (1981) 2, 188-203.

HOUTTE, J. van, C.J.M. SCHUYT, *Rechtssociologie en jurimetrie* [Sociology of law and jurimetrics]. Kluwer, Deventer, 1970.

HOUTTE, J. van, P. VINKE, Attitudes governing the acceptance of legislation among various social groups. Podgorecki, A., ed., *Knowledge and opinions about law*. London, 1973, 13-42.

HUISMAN, F., De invloed van geografische afstand op het gebruik van de kosteloze dienstverlening door het Bureau voor Rechtshulp te Assen [The influence of geographical distance on the use of free services by the Legal Aid Office of Assen]. *Rechtssociologische Mededelingen* No. 2, Groningen.

HULS, N., Het buro voor rechtshulp. Exponent van een beweging en van de beheersing daarvan [The legal aid office]. *Recht en Kritiek*, 9 (1983) 3, 343-364.

HUYSE, L., *75 miljard, om wat te doen? De justitiebegrotingen van 1966 tot 1975* [The Department of Justice Budget 1966-1975]. Acco, Leuven, 1975.

HUYSE, L., Rechtshulp en advocatuur in België. Verkenning van een moeilijke situatie [Advocates and legal aid in Belgium]. *Jura Falconis*, 12 (1976) 4, 455-458.

HUYSE, L., Sociologie van de advocatuur [The sociology of advocates]. *N.N.R.*, 3 (1980) 2, 12-29.

HUYSSE, L., De democratisering van de rechtshulp [Democratization of legal aid]. *Cahiers voor Rechtshulp*. Kluwer, 1 (1981), 17-23.

HUYSE, L., H. CAMMAER, Recrutering en selectie in de Belgische advocatuur [Recruitment and selection of Belgian advocates]. Hoekema, A., J. van Houtte, *De rechtssociologische werkkamer* [Work in progress in sociology of law]. Van Loghum Slaterus, Deventer, 1982, 41-63.

HUYSE, L., et al., Justitiebeleid in de jaren zeventig [Judical policy in the seventies]. *Res Publica*, 21 (1979) 2, 343-369.

JACOBS, T., J. van HOUTTE, Instelling, pleeggezin, gezinsbegeleiding: over opvangsystemen in de bijzondere jeugdzorg [Institution, foster family, family counseling: Reception systems in special juvenile care]. Coene, M., et al., *Het statuut van het kind* [Statute of the child]. Ced Samson, Brussel, 391-407.

JETTINGHOFF, A., Vijfenzeventig jaar Raden van Beroep [75 years of social security tribunals]. *Sociaal Maandblad Arbeid* (1977), 628-637.

JETTINGHOFF, A., Juristen en andere leken over rechtstaal en rechtspleging [Lawyers and other laypersons on legal language and adjudication]. *De Praktijkgids* (1979), 386-389.

JETTINGHOFF, A., Clients of the courts: Some data on parties in civil litigation in the Netherlands. *N.N.R.*, 4 (1983) 23.

JETTINGHOFF, A., P.J. de KONING, Zeventig jaar rechtsspraak in cijfers [Seventy years Dutch litigation in figures]. *Beleid en Maatschappij*, 3 (1976) 2, 38-44.

JETTINGHOFF, A., E. LANGERWERF, Over rechters en rechtbanken [On judges and courts]. Hoekema, A.J., J. van Houtte, *De rechtssociologische werkkamer* [Work in progress in sociology of law]. Van Loghum Slaterus, Deventer, 1982.

JETTINGHOF, A., C.J.M. SCHUYT, Recht [Law]. Rademaker, L. (red.), *Social kaart van Nederland* [Social map of the Netherlands], part 4, Kerninformatie, Aulaboeken 684. Het Spectrum, 1981, 237-269.

JETTINGHOFF, A., M.G. van WESTEROP, Over standaardkontrakten [On standard contracts]. *Mededelingen van het Juridisch Instituut van de Nederlandse Economische Hogeschool* No. 2, Rotterdam, 1973a.

JETTINGHOFF, A., M.G. van WESTEROP, Hoe komt de consument tot zijn recht? [How does the consumer realise his rights?]. *Mededelingen van het Juridisch Instituut van de Nederlandse Economische Hogeschool* No. 3, Rotterdam, 1973b.

JONGMAN, R.W., G.A.J. SMALE, De invloed van leeftijd, recidive en sociale klasse op het seponeringsbeleid [The influence of age, prior record and social class on prosecutors decisions to drop cases]. *Ned. Tijdschrift voor Criminologie* (1972), p. 30 ff.

JONGMAN, R.W., G.A.J. SMALE, Factoren die samenhangen met het seponeringsbeleid van de officier van Justitie [Factors explaining prosecutors discretion]. *Ned. Tijdschrift voor Criminologie* (1973), p. 55 ff.

KAMSTRA, O., Empirisch rechtssociologisch onderzoek: van '68 tot '80 [Empirical research in sociology of law: A survey of research from '68 to '80]. *Beleid en Maatschappij* (1980) 1, 18-25.

KAMSTRA, O., F. KUNNEMAN, Verslag van een cursus methodologie [Report on a methodology course]. *N.N.R.* (1982) 2, 118-126.

KAMSTRA, O., F. KUNNEMAN, "Hard cores" versus "main trends". On an unfruitful transplantation. *Nederlands Tijdschrift voor Rechtsfilosofie en Rechtstheorie* (1983) 3, 235-237.

KAMSTRA, O., F. KUNNEMAN, *Het expliciteren van impliciete methodologieën* [On making implicit methodologies explicit]. I.V.R. Congresbundel, Lund Zweden, December 1983, 94-107.

KAMSTRA, O., F. KUNNEMAN, Het rechtswetenschappelijk werkterrein, verkenning en verkaveling [The legal scientific working field, exploration and allocation]. *Rechtsfilosofie en Rechtstheorie*, 13 (1984) 1, 71-82.

KATE, J. ten, P.J. van KOPPEN, *Invloed van persoonskenmerken van de rechter op civielrechtelijke beslissingen* [The impact of personal characteristics of the judge on civil law decision]. Erasmus Universiteit, Rotterdam, 1982a.

KATE J. ten, P.J. van KOPPEN, De rol van juridische kennis en argumentatie bij privaatrechtelijke beslissingen [The role of juridical knowledge and argumentation in civil law decisions]. *N.N.R.* (1982b) 1, 31-51.

KAUPEN, W., E. LANGERWERF, The comparative analysis of litigation rates. Cain, M., K. Kulcsar (ed.), *Disputes and the law*. Budapest, Akademiai Kiado, 1983, 147-164.

KERCKHOVE, L. van de, L. HUYSE, Stateways cannot change folkways. Summer and Myrdal over de werkgever als inleider van sociale verandering [Stateways cannot change folkways. Summer and Myrdal on the legislator as agent of social change]. *Tijdschrift voor Sociale Wetenschappen*, 22 (1977) 2, 103-118.

KERCKHOVE, L. van de, L. HUYSE, De sociale ingenieur [The social engineer]. *Tijdschrift voor Sociale Wetenschappen*, 23 (1978) 3, 219-236.

KLIJN, A., Naamsverandering: een kwantitatieve analyse over de periode 1966-1980 [Change of name: A quantitative analysis for the period 1966-1980]. *Justitiële Verkenningen* No. 10, 1981a.

KLIJN, A., *De balie geschetst; verslag van een door het W.O.D.C. gehouden schriftelijke enquête onder de Nederlandse advokatuur [The Bar in outline; a written survey of Dutch advocates]*. Staatsuitgeverij, Den Haag, 1981b.

KLIJN, A., Van naamwijziging tot naamwetwijziging [From change of name to change of name legislation]. *Het Personeel Statuut* No. 6, 1982a.

KLIJN, A., Differentiatie en specialisatie in de balie [Differentiation and specialization at the bar]. *Advocatenblad*, 62 (1982b) 3.

KLIJN, A., *On development and prospects of social advocacy*. Ministry of Justice, The Hague, 1983a.

KLIJN, A., Die soziale Advokatur in den Niederlanden. Die Entstehung eines neuen Anwalttypes [The social advocates in the Netherlands: The genesis of a new type of advocates]. *Zeitschrift für Rechtssoziologie*, 4 (1983b) 2.

KLIJN, A., De verplichte procesvertegenwoordiging bij echtscheiding [The obliged legal proceedings representation in divorce]. *Nederlands Juristenblad*, 1 (1983c) 21, 653-660.

KLIJN, A., *Skilmesse: scheiden op zijn Deens* [Skilmesse: Divorce in a Danish way]. W.O.D.C., Den Haag, 1983d.

KLIJN, A., M.W. BOL, Naamswetgeving en naamsbeleving [Name legislation and name experience]. *Justitiële Verkenningen* No. 10, 1981.

KOLKMAN, S., The press and court proceedings. *Intermediair*, 7 (1971) 43, 9, 11, 17.

KONING, P.J. de, L.J.M. D'ANJOU, H.F.T. PENNARTS, *Het verschijnsel sociale rechtshulp* [An ideal-typical description of the phenomenon of legal aid for the poor]. Recht en Maatschappij. Kluwer, Deventer, 1983.

KONING, P.J. de, P.J. VERBERNE, Recht op privatisering? Enkele speculatieve gedachten over recht, rechtshulp, privatisering en deregulering [Some speculations on law, legal aid, privatization and deregulation]. *Recht en Kritiek*, 10 (1984) 1, 94-104.

KOOYMAN, E., Het verschijnsel van de wetswinkel [The phenomenon of law shops]. *Rechtskundig Weekblad*, 27 (1974) 35, 1929-1934.

KOPPEN, P.J. van, J. ten KATE, Use of information by the private law judge: an attributional model of judicial decision-making. *N.N.R.* (1983) 2, 262-282.

KRAAN, K.J., A. RUTTEN-ROOS, Sociologisch onderzoek en de rechtspositie van minderjarigen [Sociological research and the legal position of minors]. *Nederlands Juristenblad* (April 1978), 325-333.

LAND, R. van der, Een enquête onder de Nederlandse Rechtelijke Macht [A survey among the Dutch Legal Authority]. *Ars Aequi*, 19 (19970), 524-533.

LANGE, O.R. de, *De rol van de rechter in de samenleving* [The role of the judge in society]. W.O.D.C., Den Haag, 1977.

LANGEMEIJER, F.F., De rechtswinkels helpen 60.000 mensen per jaar [Every year the law shops help 60.000 people]. *Intermediair*, 11 (1975) 47, 1-6, 13.

LANGERWERFF, E., De invloed van de industrialisatie op de aktiviteiten van hoven en rechtbanken [The influence of industrialization on the activities of courts and tribunals, 1845-1970]. *Economisch en Sociaal Tijdschrift* (1978) 2, 215-232.

LANGERWERF, E., *De vestiging van de advokaten* [The residence of advocates]. Interuniversitair Studententijdschrift, 1979.

LANGERWERF, E., *De werkrechtersraden. Evolutie van hun werking* [The Belgian labour courts. Evolution of their activities]. Universiteit Antwerpen, 1982.

LANGERWERF, E., J. van HOUTTE, Een verklaringsmodel voor de verschillen in procesvoeringsratio van de burgerlijke rechtbanken van eerste aanleg [An explanatory model for the differences in litigation rates of the civil courts of first instance]. *Tijdschrift voor Sociale Wetenschappen* (1979) 1, 74-81.

LANGERWERF, E., F. van LOON, De opzeggingstermijnen voor bedienden in de praktijk: de rechtspraak van de Arbeidsrechtbank te Antwerpen van 1980 tot 1982 [Dismissal terms for white collars: The administration of justice of the Labour Court of Antwerp from 1980 till 1982]. *Rechtskundig Weekblad* (1983-1984), 1377-1394.

LOEFF, J.J., De list der rechtssociologie [The trick of sociology of law]. *Nederlands Juristenblad*, 46 (1971) 10, 258-270.

LOURENS, W., Hoe staat het met de sociaal-juridische hulpverlening in Rotterdam? [The socio-legal aid in Rotterdam]. *Sociaal Maandblad Arbeid* (1974), 86-98.

MAANEN, G.H.A. van, Leemte in de rechtshulp [A gap in legal aid]. *Advocatenblad*, 51 (1971) 3, 48-50.

MANEN, N. van, *De rechtshulpverleners* [Legal aid assistants]. Kluwer, Deventer, 1975.

MICHEL, G., Leemten in de rechtshulp [Gaps in legal aid]. *Rechtskundig Weekblad*, 37 (1974) 35, 1909-1922.

NIEMEIJER, E., De invloed van afstand op het gebruik van kosteloze juridische dienstverlening [The influence of distance on the use of free legal services]. *Recht en Kritiek* (1979) 3, 228-296.

NIEMEIJER, E., Review of "Bundeling van belangen bij de burgerlijke rechter" van C.A. Groenendijk [Review of "Rally of interests at the civil judge" of C.A. Groenendijk]. *N.N.R.* (1981) 2, 78-82.

NIEMEIJER, E., Review of "De sociaal-wetenschappelijke bestudering van het recht" van C.J.M. Schuyt [Review of "The socio-scientific study of legislation" of C.J.M. Schuyt]. *N.N.R.* (1982) 2, 133-139.

NIEMEIJER, E., De invloed van afstand op het gebruik van kosteloze juridische dienstverlening bij het Bureau voor Arbeidsrecht te Groningen [The influence of distance on the use of free legal aid at the Labour Legislation Office of Groningen]. *Rechtssociologische Mededelingen* No. 1, Groningen.

NIEMEIJER, E., C.M. BREEUWSMA, E. HELDER et al., *Beeld van de Arob-bezwaarschriftprocedure* [A picture of the Arob-complaint procedure]. Kluwer, Deventer, 1982.

NIEMEIJER, E., E. HELDER, Review of "Zuinig met recht" van J. Soetenhorst – De Savornin Lohmann] Review of "Economize on legislation" of J. Soetenhorst – De Savornin Lohmann]. *Recht en Kritiek* (1983) 4, 498-502.

PEPER, A., J.M.C. SCHUYT, Inleiding tot het werk van Vilhelm Aubert [Introduction to the work of Vilhelm Aubert]. *Proeven van rechtssociologie.* Universitaire Pers/Standard Wetenschappelijke Uitgeverij, Rotterdam/Antwerpen, 1971, 1-29.

PETERS, A.A.G., Maatschappelijke verandering, ouderlijke macht en recht [Social changes, parental authority and justice]. *Ars Aequi* (1976a), 12-24.

PETERS, A.A.G., Recht als vals bewustzijn [Justice as false consciousness], Kelk, C. et al., *Recht, macht en manipulatie* [Justice, power and manipulation]. Utrecht, 1976b, 189-220.

POT, M., De gebruikers van het rechtsinstituut "de omgangsregeling" [The users of the legal institute "association regulation"].

Rechtssociologische Mededelingen No. 3, Groningen, 1979.

PRAKKEN, T., De weg naar het recht: ter opvulling van de leemte in de kennis van de leemte [The road to justice]. *Nederlands Juristenblad* (1977), 216.

PRAKKEN, T., Het wrommelt in de Nederlandse rechtshulp [Something is going on in Dutch legal aid]. *Tegenspraak* (1983) 8, 374-379.

ROOS, N.N.M., Empirisch onderzoek naar het functioneren van het lekenelement [Empirical research on the functioning of lay judges]. *Justitiële Verkenningen* (1978) 23, 42-64.

ROOS, N.N.M., *Juristerij in Nederland* [Legal quibbling in the Netherlands]. Deventer, 1981a.

ROOS, N.N.M., Rol- en beslissingsgedrag van rechters [Role and decisionmaking behaviour of judges]. *Recht en Kritiek* (1981b), 402-420.

ROOS, N.N.M., *Lekenrechters* [Lay judges]. Dissertatie Nijmegen, Deventer, 1982a.

ROOS, N.N.M., Drie oraties: ideologie, kritiek en relativering (Van Seeters, Crombag, Blankenburg) [Three orations: Ideology, criticism and relativation (Van Seeters, Crombag, Blankenburg)]. *N.N.R.* (1982b) 1, 98-103.

ROOS, N.N.M., Webers view concerning lay adjudication. *N.N.R.* (1983a) 2, 3767-391, paper for the congress of the European Research Committee on Sociology of Law. Antwerp, September 1983a.

ROOS, N.N.M., Summary of lekenrechters [Lay Judges]. *N.n.R.* (1983b) 2, 392-402.

SCHEFFER, W.C.M., L. WOLDDRINGH, H.H.J.M. KNAPEN, *De rechtspositie van minderjarigen* [The legal position of minors]. Instituut voor Toegepaste Sociologie, Nijmegen, 1977.

SCHILT, T., R.W. JONGMAN, Het seponeringsbeleid opnieuw bekeken [Prosecutors' discretion revisited]. *Ned. Tijdschrift voor Crimonologie* (1976), p. 238 ff.

SCHREINER, A., Om- en terugkeer van de eigendom [Turn and return of property]. *Alibi*, 14 (1984) 3, 29-31.

SCHUYT, C.J.M., Problemen van rechtssociologisch onderzoek [Problems of socio-legal research]. Van Houtte, J., C.J.M. Schuyt et al., *Rechtssociologie en jurimetrie* [Sociology of law and jurimetrics]. Kluwer, Deventer, 1970a.

91

SCHUYT, C.J.M., *Attitudes towards new socio-economic legislation, a before-after experiment on the normative effects of the introduction of the tax added value*, Varna, World Congress of Sociology, 1970a, also published in: Schelsky, H., M. Rehbinder, *Jahrbuch für Rechtssoziologie und Rechtstheorie*, Band 3, Zur Effektivität des Rechts. Bertelmann Verlag, 565-596, 1973.

SCHUYT, C.J.M., Stagiaires [The lawyer-apprentices]. *Advocatenblad*, October, 1970a.

SCHUYT, C.J.M., Problemen rond het rechtssociologisch onderzoek [Problems concerning socio-legal research]. Van Houtte, J., J.C.M. Schuyt, *Rechtssociologie en jurimetrie* [Sociology of law and jurimetrics]. Kluwer, Deventer, 1970b, 43-57.

SCHUYT, C.J.M., *Een introductie in de rechtssociologie aan de hand van het werk van Vilhelm Aubert* [Essays in sociology of law from the work of Vilhelm Aubert]. Universitaire Pers, Rotterdam, 1971a.

SCHUYT, C.J.M., *Rechtssociologie, een terreinverkenning* [Sociology of law, an introduction]. Universitaire Pers, Rotterdam, 1971b.

SCHUYT, C.J.M., Rechtshulp in sociologisch perspectief [Legal aid from a sociological point of view]. *Rechtshulp in Nederland, de leemte in de Balie opgevuld?* [Legal aid in the Netherlands, the gap in the Bar filled up?]. *J.S.V.V.-bulletin* (June, 1971c), 60-67.

SCHUYT, C.J.M., *Recht, orde en burgerlijke ongehoorzaamheid* [Law, social order and civil disobedience]. De Universitaire Pers, Rotterdam, 1972.

SCHUYT, C.J.M., Is burgerlijke ongehoorzaamheid in Nederland gerechtvaardigd? [Civil disobedience in the Netherlands justified?]. Kernvragen, *Tijdschrift van het Onderwijsdepartement van het Ministerie van Landsverdediging*. Den Haag, 1973a.

SCHUYT, C.J.M., Rechtshulp en democratie [Legal aid and democracy]. *Jaarlijks Rapport van de Wetswinkels*. Groningen, 1973b.

SCHUYT, C.J.M., Commentaar op het "Rapport over rechtshulp door de Nederlandse balie" [Comment on the "Report on legal aid by the Dutch Bar Association]. *Advocatenblad* (1973).

SCHUYT, C.J.M., Rechtshulp: individuele of gemeenschapszaak? 38 stellingen over de hervorming van de rechtshulp in de sociale/niet-commerciële sektor [Legal aid: A private or public cause? 38 propositions on the reorganisation of legal aid in the social/non-commercial sector]. *Advocatenblad*, 53 (1973d) 7, 403-411.

SCHUYT, C.J.M., *Rechtvaardigheid en effectiviteit in de verdeling van levenskansen; een rechtssociologische beschouwing* [Justice and effectiveness in the life chances distribution; a socio-legal approach]. De Universitaire Pers, Rotterdam, 1973e.

SCHUYT, C.J.M., Justieel beleid en wetenschappelijk onderzoek [Judicial policy and scientific research]. *Beleid en Maatschappij* (1973), 22-29.

SCHUYT, C.J.M., Normen en feiten in de rechtssociologie [Facts and values in sociology of law]. *Rechtsphilosophie en Rechtstheorie*, 3 (1974a) 1, 1-31.

SCHUYT, C.J.M., De stagiaire van 1973. Verslag van een enquête [The lawyer-apprentices in 1973. A survey report]. *Advocatenblad* (1974b), 473-490.

SCHUYT, C.J.M., Achterstand van het recht: een beleidsprobleem, [Abidence to the law: A policy problem]. *Beleid en Maatschappij* (1975a).

SCHUYT, C.J.M., Sociologie en morele overtuiging [Sociology and moral opinion]. *Intermediair* (October, 1975b).

SCHUYT, C.J.M., De sociale toekomst van de verzorgingsstaat [The future of the welfare state]. *Beleid en Maatschappij* (July/Aug., 1976a).

SCHUYT, C.J.M., De opinies van leken over klasse-justitie [Lay opinions on class justice]. *De Gids*, No. 9-10 1976b.

SCHUYT, C.J.M., The self-created conflict: Civil disobedience in the United States and in the Netherlands compared. *Criminology between the rule of law and the outlaws*. Volume in honour of W.H. Nagel. Kluwer. Deventer, 1976c.

SCHUYT, C.J.M., B.M. BLEGVAD, C.M. CAMPBELL (ed.), *European Yearbook on law and sociology*. Martinus Nijhoff, The Hague, 1977a.

SCHUYT, C.J.M., Rechtshulp en conflictoplossing [Legal aid and conflict settlement]. *Rechtshulp*, 1 (1977b) 5.

SCHUYT, C.J.M., Rechtssociologie [Sociology of law]. *Nederlandse Sociologische Encyclopedie*. Utrecht, 1977c.

SCHUYT, C.J.M., Recente literatuur over problemen van wetgeving [Recent literature on the study of legislation]. *Beleid en Maatschappij* (July, 1977d).

SCHUYT, C.J.M., Access to the legal system and legal services research. *European Yearbook on Law and Sociology*. The Hague, 1977e.

SCHUYT, C.J.M., Sociale achtergronden van de Rechten van de Mens en de schending van deze rechten [Social backgrounds of Human Rights and human rights violations]. *Amnesty Internationals' Publications*. Amsterdam, 1977f.

SCHUYT, C.J.M., Problemen van wetgeving [Problems of legislation]. *Beleid en Maatschappij*, 4 (1977g) 7/8, 186-197.

SCHUYT, C.J.M., Juristische Problemen wie private Problemen, die Verteilung von Rechtshilfe in den Niederlanden [Legal problems as well as private problems: the distribution of legal services in the Netherlands]. *Jahrbuch für Rechtssociologie und Rechtstheorie*, Band 5. Bertelmann Verlag, 1978a.

SCHUYT, C.J.M., Paradigmatische vernieuwingen in rechtsleer en rechtswetenschap [Paradigmatic innovations in jurisprudence and legal science]. *Proceedings of the Lustrum Conference*. School of Economics, Tilburg, 1978b.

SCHUYT, C.J.M., De eiser voor sociale zekerheidsrechtbanken [The claimant before social security tribunals]. *Nederlands Gerechtelijk Tijdschrift*, 2 (1979a) 1.

SCHUYT, C.J.M., De fragmentering van de overheidsadministratie in de verzorgingsstaat [The fragmentation of public administration in the welfare state]. *Mens en Maatschappij* (1979b), 33-45.

SCHUYT, C.J.M., Paradigmatische vernieuwing in de rechtswetenschap [Paradigmatic renewal in legal science]. *Ars Aequi* (December 1979c), 235-245.

SCHUYT, C.J.M., *Recht en samenleving* [Law and society]. Gorcum, Assen, 1981a.

SCHUYT, C.J.M., De overbelasting van rechtbanken [The workload of the judiciary]. *Trema* (March 1981b).

SCHUYT, C.J.M., Burgerlijke ongehoorzaamheid op zaterdag [Civil disobedience on saturday]. *Wending* (April 1981c).

SCHUYT, C.J.M., Schending van de "Mensenrechten", sociale achtergronden [Violations of human rights, societal backgrounds]. *Internationale Spectator* (October, 1981d).

SCHUYT, C.J.M., De verzorgingsstaat ter discussie [The welfare state in discussion]. *De Volkskrant* (May 7-8, 1981e).

SCHUYT, C.J.M., Ongeregeldheden, inaugurele rede, Staatsuniversiteit Leiden [Irregulars in the present, inaugural address, State Univeristy

Leyden], Samson, Alphen a/d Rijn, 1982a.

SCHUYT, C.J.M., De sociaal-wetenschappelijke bestudering van het recht [The social science approach to law]. Wolff-Albers, A.D., H.F.M. Crombag, *Visies op onderzoek in enkele sociale wetenschappen* [Research in social sciences]. Ministerie van Onderwijs, Den Haag, 1982b.

SCHUYT, C.J.M., Burgers tussen normen en rechten [Citizens between rules and judges]. Ringeling, A., J. van de Geest, A. Oosting, Administratie tussen normen en rechters [Administration between rules and judges]. Samson, Alphen a.d. Rijn, 1982c.

SCHUYT, C.J.M., *Burgerlijke ongehoorzaamheid in Nederland: 1968-1982*, [Civil disobedience in the Netherlands: 1968-1982]. Zutphen, 1982d.

SCHUYT, C.J.M., Bezuinigen in de rechtshulp? [Cutbacks in legal aid?]. *Duur recht is geen recht* [Expensive law isn't law]. Vereniging Rechtshulp, Amsterdam, 1982e.

SCHUYT, C.J.M., *Tussen macht en moraal, over de plaats van het recht in verzorgingsstaat en democratie* [Between power and morals, the place of law in the welfare state]. Samson, Alphen a.d. Rijn, 1983a.

SCHUYT, C.J.M., De betekenis van de verzorgingsstaat: verdelend recht en economische crisis [The meaning of the welfare state: Distributive justice and the economic crisis]. Veldkamp, G.J.M. (ed.), *Social security in the eighties*. Kluwer, Deventer, 1983b.

SCHUYT, C.J.M., H.D. Thoreau en burgerlijke ongehoorzaamheid [H.D. Thoreau and civil disobedience]. *Trema* (March, 1983c).

SCHUYT, C.J.M., De handen en voeten van het beleid: vage begrippen bij staatsinterventie [The role of vague concepts in the welfare state]. Van Doorn, J.A.A., J.W. De Beus (eds.), *De interventiestaat* [The interventionist state]. Boom, Meppel, 1984.

SCHUYT, C.J.M., C.A. GROENENDIJK, B.P. SLOOT, *De weg naar het recht* [Access to the legal system, a socio-legal research into unmet legal needs]. Kluwer, Deventer, 1976.

SCHUYT, C.J.M., C.A. GROENENDIJK, B.P. SLOOT, Access to the legal systems and legal services research. Blegvad, B., C.M. Campbell, C.J.M. Schuyt, *European Yearbook on Law and Sociology*. Martinus Nijhoff, The Hague, 1977, 98-121.

SCHUYT, C.J.M., A. JETTINGHOFF, F. ZWART, *Een beroep op de rechter. Een verkennend onderzoek naar de ervaringen van burgers met rechtspraak in het sociale-verzekeringsrecht, met name inzake de ziektewet, de werkloosheidswet en de wet op de arbeidsongeschiktheidsverzekering* [Social security claims before tribunals 1903-1978. An explorative study of the experiences of citizens, with jurisdiction in social security law]. Kluwer, Deventer, 1978.

SCHUYT, C.J.M., E. van de BEEK, G. ENGBERSEN et al., *Rechtshulp in wetswinkels en bevolkingsadviesbureaus* [Legal aid in legal aid bureaux and citizens advice bureaux]. Ministry of Welfare Publications, Den Haag, 1984.

SLOOT, B.P., Positieve discriminatie en de Amerikaanse grondwet [Positive discrimination and the U.S. Constitution]. *Nederlands Juristenblad* (1979), 597-608

SLOOT, B.P., *Ervaringen van vrouwelijke juristen* [Experiences of women-lawyers]. Nijmegen, 1980a.

SLOOT, B.P., Officiële uitsluiting van vrouwen in juridische beroepen [Official exclusion of women in legal professions]. *Nederlands Juristenblad* (1980b), 1186-1194.

SLOOT, B.P., Legitimatie van positieve discriminatie. Twee redeneerpatronen [Legitimation of positive discrimination: Two patterns of reasoning]. *Ars Aequi* (1981), 655-683.

SLOOT, B.P., The Equal Rights Amendment. *Nederlands Juristenblad* (1984).

SMITS, R.J., Hoe (on)geloofwaardig is P.H. Bakker Schut? [On the (un)credibility of a certain lawyer, Bakker Schut]. *Wetenschap en Samenleving*, 32 (1978) 2, 62-63.

SMITS, R.J., Juridisch-sociale indicatoren? [On socio-legal indicators]. *N.N.R.* (1979) 1, 33-43.

SMITS, R.J., Enkele problemen van wetgeving [Some problems of legislation]. *N.N.R.* (1981) 2, 34-49.

SMITS, R.J., Wat aandacht voor een juridische wees. Een notitie over tuchtrecht [A note on disciplinary law]. *N.N.R.* (1982a) 1, 58-69.

SMITS, R.J., Enkele problemen van wetgeving – 2 [Some problems of legislation, part two]. *N.N.R.* (1982b) 2, 105-117.

SMITS, R.J., Several book reviews and book notes, published in: *N.N.R.* (1979, No. 1; 1980, No. 1 and 2; 1981, No. 1). *De Sociologische Gids*

(1982, No. 1; 1983, No. 3/4), *Mens en Maatschappij* (1983, No. 2 and 3).

SMITS, R.J. Boekbesprekingen. Is er een minimum-moraal? [On the norms in science and book reviewing]. *Sociologische Gids*, 31 (1984) 3 (forthcoming).

SMITS, R.J., A. KLIJN, De ongehoorzame burger [The disobedient citizen]. *Intermediair*, 11 (1975a) 42, 1, 3, 5.

SMITS, R.J., A. KLIJN, Repliek op C.J.M. Schuyt [Reply to Schuyt]. *Intermediair*, 11 (1975b) 42, 13.

SNEL, B., *Kijken in de rechtzaal – een observatieonderzoek naar buitenjuridische factoren die ter zitting het vonnis van de politierechter beïnvloeden* [Courtroom observation – an analysis of the extra judicial factors which influence the decision of police-judges]. Samson, Alphen a.d. Rijn, 1977.

SNIJDERS, H.J., *Rechtsvinding door de burgerlijke rechter – een kwantitatief rechtspraakonderzoek bij de Hoge Raad en Gerechtshoven* [Finding of the law by civil court judges – a quantitative research of decisions by Appelate and Higher Courts]. Kluwer, Deventer, 1978.

SNOEK, A., De correspondenten van het bureau voor arbeidsrecht [The correspondents of the bureau of Labour Law]. *Recht en Kritiek* (1980) 4, 489-495.

SNOEK, A., Korrespondenten van het Bureau voor Arbeidsrecht te Groningen. Eerstelijns rechtshulpverleners, vroeger en nu [Correspondents of the Labour Legislation Office of Groningen. First line legal assistance, past and present]. *Rechtssociologische Mededelingen* No. 4, Groningen.

SNOEK, A., E. HEKMAN, "Spreekt de pastor een woordje mee?" De invloed van de pastores in de gemeente Groningen op de totstandkoming van een bezoekregeling bij echtscheiding [The influence of the pastors in Groningen on the establishment of a visiting regulation after divorce]. *Rechtssociologische Mededelingen* No. 5, Groningen.

SOETENHORST-de SAVORNIN LOHMAN, J., *Zuinig met recht* [Law as a scarce resource]. Sociaal en Cultureel Planbureau, Rijswijk, 1983.

TIGGES, L.C.M., E.C.M. NUIJTEN-EDELBRUCH, *De vraaghulp in praktijk gebracht* [The reality of social work in court]. W.O.D.C., Den Haag, 1981.

TULKENS, J.J.J., G.A. van BERGEIJK, *Vervolgingsbeleid* [Prosecution policy]. W.O.D.C., Den Haag, 1972.

VERWOERD, J.R.A., *De herziening van de rechterlijke macht in België* [Reorganisation of the judiciary in Belgium]. Staatsuitgeverij, Den Haag, 1978.

VERWOERD, J.R.A., *De Justizreform in de Bondsrepubliek Duitsland* [Judicial reform in the Federal Republic of Germany]. Staatsuitgeverij, Den Haag, 1980.

VERWOERD, J.R.A., *Enkelvoudige en meervoudige kamers in burgerlijke zaken bij de arrondissementsrechtbanken* [Single chambers and full benches in civil cases in the district courts]. W.O.D.C., Den Haag, 1981.

VERWOERD, J.R.A., Gerechtelijke reorganisatie in veranderd perspectief: België, de Bondsrepubliek Duitsland en Nederland [Judicial reorganisation in a changed perspective: Belgium, the Federal Republic of Germany and the Netherlands]. *Tegenspraak* No. 4, 1982.

VERWOERD, J.R.A., De rechtsverzorgingsstaat in discussie [The legal welfare state in discussion]. *Nederlands Juristenblad*, 11 (1983), 336-340.

VINKE, P., Wat is en waarom rechtssociologie? [Definition and function of sociology of law]. Van Houtte, J., CJM Schuyt, *Rechtssociologie en jurimetrie* [Sociology of law and jurimetrics]. Kluwer, Deventer, 1970.

VINKE, P., De relevantie van de rechtssociologie in de moderne geïndustrialiseerde samenleving en haar institutionalisering als interdisciplinaire wetenschap [The relevance of sociology of law in the modern industrialized society and its institutionalization as interdisciplinary science]. *Mens en Maatschappij*, 47 (1972), 197-218.

VINKE, P., Norm en praktijk van de moderne belastingwetgeving betreffende inkomsten en vermogen [Norms and practice of modern taxation legislation concerning income and property]. *Weekblad Fiscaal Recht* (1982).

VINKE, P., I.J. BERGHUIS-van der WIJK, Houding van directeuren grote naamloze vennootschappen ten aanzien van enkele aspecten van belastingheffen. Een rechtssociologische benadering. [The attitude of directors of large limited liability companies concerning certain aspects of taxation. A socio-legal approach]. *Acta Politica* (1971), 269-282.

VINKE, P., I.J. BERGHUIS-van der WIJK, *Rechtsregels in de*

ervaringswereld van verschillende bevolkingslagen [The attitudes of different population groups concerning legal norms]. Kluwer, Deventer, 1975.

VOCHT, C. de, R. VERHOEVEN, J. van HOUTTE, *Onderhoudsplichtige mannen en onderhoudsgerechtigde vrouwen* [Men obliged to provide maintenance and wives entitled to obtain maintenance]. Kluwer, Deventer, 1978.

VRIES, G. de, *Sociale orde, regels en de sociologie* [Social order, rules and sociology]. Boom, Meppel, 1977.

WERFF, C. van der, Opvattingen over echtscheiding en alimentatie [Public opinion concerning divorce and alimony]. *Justitiële Verkenningen* No. 5, 1981.

WERFF, C. van der, C. COZIJN, *Opvattingen over de alimentatieduur* [Opinions on the duration of alimony payments]. Staatsuitgeverij, Den Haag, 1983.

WICHERS-HOETH, L., De balie, een leemte in de rechtshulp? [The Bar, a gap in legal aid?]. *Advocatenblad*, 50 (1970) 8, 349-359.

WICHERS-HOETH, L., De balie. Een leemte in de rechtshulp [The traditional advocay. Gaps in legal aid]. *Ars Aequi*, 19 (1970) 6, 225-313 (special issue).

WICHERS-HOETH, L., De Rechtshulp in België. Verslag van het Rechtshulpcongres te Leuven, 12-13 maart 1976 [Legal aid in Belgium. Report of the Legal Aid Congress in Louvain, march 1976]. *Jura Falconis*, 12 (1975-1976) 4, 419-531 (special issue).

ZOMER, O.J., *De strafvervolging en straftoemeting in gevallen van zware criminaliteit* [Charging and pleading in felony cases]. W.O.D.C., Den Haag, 1981.

ZUIDEMA, H., E. HEKMAN, "Neemt de agent de wijk bij echtscheiding?" De rol van de politie bij de totstandkoming van een bezoekregeling bij echtscheiding [The role of the police in the establishment of a visiting regulation after divorce]. *Rechtssociologische Mededelingen*, No. 7, Groningen.

ZUIDEMA, H., E. HEKMAN, De rol van het onderwijs bij de totstandkoming van een bezoekregeling bij echtscheiding [The role of the educational institutions in the establishment of a visiting regulation after divorce]. *Rechtssociologische Mededelingen*, No. 9, Groningen.

Systematical order

Law, legislation

D'Anjou (1982), von Benda-Beckmann and Strijbosch (1984), Blankenburg (1980b, 1982a), Bos (1970a, 1972, 1976ab), Bruinsma (1978), Griffiths (1978a, 1979ab, 1980, 1981, 1983a, 1984a), van Groenendael (1983), Hoekema and Huppes (1978), Niemeijer and Helder (1983), Peters (1976b), Prakken (1977), Schuyt (1977dg, 1981a, 1983ab), Schuyt et al. (1976), Sloot (1981), Smits (1981, 1982b), Soetenhorst-de Savornin Lohman (1983).

Sociology of law and socio-legal research

D'Anjou (1978), Blankenburg (1983ab), Blegvad et al. (1978), Bos (1970b, 1975b, 1978, 1980, 1982), Bruinsma (1980, 1983a), Cozijn (1983), Griffiths (1984b), Hoekema (1970b, 1973, 1974, 1978b, 1979, 1980b, 1982), Hoekema and van Houtte (1982), van Houtte (1970ab, 1971, 1975), van Houtte and Dierickx (1970, 1971), van Houtte and Schuyt (1970), Jettinghof and Schuyt (1981), Kamstra (1980, 1982), Kamstra and Kunneman (1983, 1984), van de Kerckhove and Huyse (1977), Loeff (1971), Niemeijer (1982), Peper and Schuyt (1971), Roos (1983a), Schuyt (1970d, 1971ab, 1973, 1974a, 1977c, 1978b, 1979c, 1982a), Schuyt et al. (1977a), Smits (1979), Vinke (1970, 1972), de Vries (1977).

Knowledge and opinion about law

Hoekema (1971, 1975a, 1976a), van Houtte (1973), van Houtte et al. (1983), van Houtte and Vinke (1973), Jettinghof (1979), Schuyt (1972, 1973a, 1975b, 1976bc, 1981c, 1982b, 1983c), Smits (1984), Smits and Klijn (1975a), Vinke and Berghuis-van der Wijk (1975).

The bar: Selection and organisation

Bakker-van der A (1970), Berends (1979), Berghuis-van der Wijk (1982), van

Braam and Surie (1972), Claessens et al. (1970), Dassen and van der Heyden (1978), Griffiths (1978b), van Groenendael (1973), van Houtte (1974), van Houtte and Langerwerf (1976), Hoevels and Krynen (1974), Hooftman (1976), Huyse (1976, 1980), Huyse and Cammaer (1982), Klijn (1981b, 1982b, 1983ab), Langerwerf (1979), Roos (1981a), Schuyt (1970c, 1974b), Sloot (1980ab).

Legal system: Legal organisation, judicial decision making, adjudication, class justice, judicial policy, dispute settlement

Blankenburg (1980a, 1982b), Blankenburg and Fiedler (1981), Blankenburg and Reifner (1982), Blankenburg and Rogowsky (1983), Blankenburg et al. (1982, 1983), Broekman and 't Hart (1980), Bruinsma (1983b), Crombag et al. (1977), van Duyne (1983), Glastra van Loon (1984), Gras (1982a), Griffiths (1983b), Groenendijk (1975ab, 1981b, 1982a), Hoefnagels (1970), Hoekema (1976c, 1978a), Houtappel (1978), van Houtte (1983abc), van Houtte and Langerwerf (1977ab, 1977-'78, '78-'79), van Houtte et al. (1981), Huyse (1975), Huyse et al. (1979), Jettinghof (1977, 1983), Jettinghof and de Koning (1976), Jettinghof and Langerwerf (1982), ten Kate and van Koppen (1982ab), Kaupen and Langerwerf (1983), Kolkman (1971), van Koppen and Ten Kate (1983), van der Land (1970), de Lange (1977), Langerwerf (1978, 1982), Langerwerf and van Houtte (1979), Langerwerf and van Loon (1983-'84), Niemeijer (1981), Niemeijer et al. (1982), Roos (1978, 1981b, 1982a, 1983b), Schuyt (1973f, 1975a, 1977e, 1979a, 1981b), Schuyt et al. (1977, 1978), Snel (1977), Snijders (1978), Snoek (1980), Tigges and Nuyten-Edelbruck (1981), Verwoerd (1978, 1980, 1981, 1982, 1983).

Legal aid

van de Beek et al. (1983), Bergma and Verberne (1974), Blankenburg (1983c, 1984), Blankenburg and Cooper (1982), Boekman (1972 and '77), Breda (1983), Breda et al. (1981abcde), Duintjer-Klein (1976), Frid (1976), Geerst (1977), Gils (1972), Griffiths (1977), van Groenendael and van der Vaart (1983), van Groenendael et al. (1971), Groenendijk (1974, 1978, 1981a,

1983b), Groenendijk et al. (1975, 1976), Hannema (1983), Hes (1982, 1983), van den Heuvel (1974), Huls (1983), Huyse (1981), de Koning et al. (1983), de Koning and Verberne (1984), Kooyman (1974), Langermeijer (1975), Laurens (1974), van Maanen (1971), van Manen (1975), Michel (1974), Niemeijer (1979), Prakken (1983), Schuyt (1971c, 1973bcd, 1977b, 1978a, 1982d), Schuyt et al. (1984), Wichers-Hoeth (1970), X (1970), X (1975-1976).

Specific legal institutions

Marriage, family and divorce

Cozijn (1978b, 1981, 1982), Cozijn and van der Werff (1981), Griffiths (1983c), Gysels and Vogels (1982), Gysels et al. (1984), van Houtte (1980, 1982a), van Houtte and Bax (1979), van Houtte and de Vocht (1978, 1981-'82), Klijn (1983cd), Pot (1979), de Vocht et al. (1978).

Juvenile care, legal position of minors, parental authority, protection of minors, adoption, maintenance between parents and their adult children

Berckmans et al. (1981), van Houtte (1977, 1982b, 1983d), van Houtte and Breda (1976, 1978), Jacobs and van Houtte (1980), Kraan and Rutten-Roos (1978), Peters (1976a), Scheffer et al. (1977), Smits (1982a).

Property law, obligations, contracts and settlement of damages

van der Borght (1978), Cozijn (1978a), Goedmakers (1980), Gras (1979, 1980, 1982b, 1983ab), Hoekema (1976b, 1980a), Jettinghof and van Westrop (1973a), Schreiner (1984).

Immigration legislation

Groenendijk (1973b, 1979, 1981c, 1982b, 1983acd), Groenendijk and Swart (1975, 1978), Groenendijk et al. (1982), Havinga (1983).

Fiscal law: Tax added value and taxation

Berghuis-van der Wijk et al. (1970), van Houtte and Callens (1977), van Houtte and Langerwerf (1978-'80, 1981, 1983), Schuyt (1973), Vinke (1982), Vinke and Berghuis-van der Wijk (1971).

Other: Name and traffic legislation, consumer law, privacy, passport legislation, human rights, social and public institutions

Bloembergen et al. (1972), Bloembergen and van Wersch (1973), Bol and Klijn (1981), Cozijn (1977), van Doorn and Schuyt (1978), Franken (1973), Groenendijk (1973a), Hoekema (1975bc, 1978c), Jettinghof and van Westerop (1973b), Klijn (1981a, 1982a), Klijn and Bol (1981), Schuyt (1973e, 1977f, 1979b, 1981de, 1982, 1984), Sloot (1979, 1984).

PART TWO

Legal anthropology

Current legal anthropology in the Netherlands: Trend report*

J. GRIFFITHS

The historical background of modern Dutch anthropology of law[1]

The adat-law school

A birthdate as good as any other for Dutch anthropology of law is 3 October 1901, the day on which Cornelis van Vollenhoven delivered his inaugural lecture at the University of Leiden as professor of constitutional and administrative law of the Dutch overseas territories and of the adat-law of the Dutch East Indies. Although the study of adat-law (the unwritten indigenous law of much of Southeast Asia) certainly did not begin with van Vollenhoven (see van Vollenhoven, 1928; Sonius, 1976) it was he who by general consent "elevated the study of adat-law to a *science*" (van Ossenbruggen, 1933: 1). During the next four decades, van Vollenhoven and his disciples produced an imposing body of descriptive and theoretical

---

* This article is a greatly shortened version of one which first appeared in 1983/2 *Nieuwsbrief voor Nederlandstalige Rechtssociologen* and was presented at the 1983 joint meeting of the Research Committee on Sociology of Law (ISA) and the Vereniging voor de Sociaal-wetenschappelijke bestudering van het Recht, in Antwerp. Unlike the full version, it makes no pretention to bibliographic or other all-inclusiveness. The persons acknowledged in the original version for their contributions to it bear no responsibility for the selection presented here; I would, however, like to express my gratitude to K. von Benda-Beckmann for her advice and help in this regard. All translations from Dutch originals are my own. A somewhat different version of the original is Griffiths (1985a).
[1] The early history of legal anthroplogy in other countries is discussed in: Schott 91982) – Germany; Negri (1978) – Italy; Vanderlinden (1978) – Belgium; Strijbosch (1978) – the Netherlands; Snyder (1981a), Roberts (1979: ch. 22), Moore (1970), Nader (1965) – England and the United States.

writing concerning adat-law.[2] F. von Benda-Beckmann (1981b: 298) observes of this vast intellectual productivity:

> In the first four decades of the twentieth century no other country in the world equally the Netherlands and the former Dutch East Indien in the quantity of legal-ethnographic material collected and analyzed ... or in the number and quality of legal-ethnographic monographs.

The focus of the adat-law school was on the rules and instituions of adat-law. The major part of the production of van Vollenhoven and his disciples consisted of detailed compilations and analysis of the law of the various 'legal areas' of what is now Indonesia. In putting rules at the center of the study of law, the adat-law school was typical of anthropology of law generally before the second world war. Philosophical and legal conceptions undoubtedly played a part in this concentration on rules, but the specific colonial context of legal anthropology's early years was also important. Every colonial system had to confront the question of legal order in the colonial territories and in particular the question of the relative places of the existing (largely indigenous) law and of the law of the colonial power. This question, generally posed in terms of the relative competence of competing systems of rules and institutions, was widely (and justly) regarded as touching the heart of the political and social relations between the colonial power, the local political and legal authorities, and the population at large. It therefore attracted a great deal of often quite heated attention, a fact of the political context by which anthropologists were not unaffected. The politics of colonialism, in short, defined to a large extent the research agenda for legal anthropology in a way which put the focus upon the rules and institutions of the colonized peoples.

In the case of the adat-law school, the colonial context is not only of a general background relevance: it furnished several major political controversies within which van Vollenhoven and his disciples adopted pronounced political positions. Two controversies in particular had immediate consequences for the theoretical and practical orientation of adat-law studies: the repeated proposals to unify the substantive law

---

[2]   The work of van Vollenhoven and the adat-law school is discussed in Strijbosch (1980), Sonius (1976), and Holleman (1981a). See ter Haar (1948: 234-248) for a bibliography.

applicable in the Dutch East Indies (see Sonius, 1976; Strijbosch, 1980: 30-37), and the question to what extent the adat-law claims of local communities to 'unused' land could be considered equivalent to 'ownership' and therefore exempted from declarations of state dominion over 'unowned' land (see F. von Benda -Beckmann, 1982b: 2; Sonius, 1976: 40-42). In both cases, van Vollenhoven and his disciples emphasized the integrity and distinct character of the adat-law systems. In their view, this entitled those systems to a measure of political and intellectual respect which was inconsistent both with the imperialistic pretention implicit in the notion that unitary law along Dutch lines would necessarily be better for the local population and with the juridical ethnocentrism of the notion that only one form of 'ownership' can be known to the law.

If the context of colonial rule set the stage and largely determined the action which would appear scientifically relevant to legal anthropologists, van Vollenhoven and his disciples threw themselves into their work as observers and analysts which a self-conscious wish to be of service to the production. In the most general terms, they expected that the scientific study of non-western law in a comparative, historical perspective would be a "powerful medicine against the intellectual self-centeredness and chauvinism ... which so often stand in the way of insight into and understanding of another society – with a different nature and background – and its laws" (Holleman, 1981a: 18, quoting van Asbeck). Such a science would be able, in Holleman's words, "to point out the wrongs entailed in existing or proposed law, to clear away misconceptions concerning other sorts of law, and to expose dogmatic prejudices" (1981a: 18). But there was a more immediate purpose as well:

> Our objective is not the study of adat-law in itself ...; our highest objective is to bring about an administration of justice and a system of governance which is not just good on paper but also in reality ... two things which cannot be attained without a solid knowledge of local law and opinion. (van Vollenhoven, 1909: 90).

While the primary focus of van Vollenhoven and the adat-law school was on rules and institutions, they certainly did not go about their work in a narrow, formalistic way. The 'law' they were interested in was not a list of ideally-applicable rules, but law-in-action. In principle, it was to be collected by means of what Hoebel (1954: 34-35) has called the "descriptive method", in which the rules of law are extracted not from answers to abstract questions about 'what the law is', but from observation of, and questions addressed to, actual practice: decisions, trouble cases, patterns of interaction, etc. (see Strijbosch, 1980: 81-84).[3]

A few of the central themes and concepts of the adat-law school deserve mention here, especially because of their relevance for more recent developments in legal anthropology. In the first place, the concept of 'law': van Vollenhoven initially defined adat-law as "that collection of operative rules of behavior which on the one hand are enforced by sanctions (hence 'law') and on the other hand are uncodified (hence 'adat')" (1918: 14). He acknowledged that no strict distinction between law and other social control could be drawn in practice and he was inclined to dismiss the conceptual question concerning the nature of law as mere "theorizing" (see Holleman, 1981a: 24). In fact, however, enforcement was not the operative criterion in the work of the adat-law school, but rather specialized authorities. In the theoretical reformulation of the concept of adat-law by ter Haar, this took the form of the so-called *beslissingenleer* (decision theory). Anticipating Pospisil's (1971) well-known formulation of the concept of law by more than 30 years, ter Haar argued that:

> Adat-law can only be known from the decisions of authoritative functionaries of the group (headmen, judges, popular assemblies, guardians of the land, religious and villages officials), which are rendered either with respect to a dispute or otherwise ... (1937: 5).[4]

---

[3] Hoebel (1954: 33) wrongly characterizes the work of the adat-law school as exemplifying the 'ideological' method (in which the rules prevailing in a social group are established by asking for abstract statements about what the law of the group is). See generally Strijbosch (1980). Strijbosch also discusses ter Haar's argument that the object of study should be limited to rules exemplified in decisions of authorities; Strijbosch argues (1980: 70-79) that this should be regarded as a programmatic statement, since it is not descriptive of the actual work of the adat-law school. See note 4 below for further discussion of ter Haar's position.

[4] This statement of the *beslissingenleer* was set in the context of ter Haar's programmatic statement of the position of adat-law scholarship as a form of positive legal science rather than an ethnographic one. It was rejected by other adat-law scholars who were of the opinion that rules which *could be* sanctioned, and not only those for which actual examples of sanctioning could be cited, deserved to be treated as legal. See Holleman (1981a: 24-25; cf. also 1973: 592).

As early as the 1920s the concepts of "authoritatively 'attested' or 'supported' ... law observance (*gesteunde naleving*) and of 'preventive law care' (*preventieve rechtszorg*)" had been formulated by adat-law scholars to describe the behavior of adat functionaries "aimed at removing legal uncertainty and avoiding ... the prospect of future disputes" (Holleman, 1973: 594). The adat requirement that various important legal transactions (marriage, land transfer, etc.) take place in the presence of specified local functionaries seemed plainly 'legal' in character but not easily subsumed under a concept of law conceived in terms of conflicts and sanctions. A concept of law applicable to what Holleman later called "trouble-less cases" was needed. The resulting idea of "preventive law care" can be put to much more general use than the study of Indonesian adat-law, however: a sociological analysis of the function of the Notary, for example, would be impossible without it (cf. Cohen, 1958, 1970). Until recently, the sociology and anthropology of law have had very few sources of analytic insight into legal phenomena from which the element of enforceability is lacking or (largely) irrelevant other than the works of the adat-law school (see Holleman, 1973).

If the adat-law scholars were in several respects ahead of their time as far as the analysis of the concept of law is concerned, the same is true of their conception of the nature of the social groups which can be said to have law. Within the context of his universal, comparative method, built up – by analogy to linguistics – out of larger and smaller circles of legal affinity, van Vollenhoven considered the "legal community" (*rechtsgmeenschap*) as the fundamental social locus of law (1901: 5). Holleman (1981a: 19) describes the concept as follows:

> These are loosely or tightly bound groups with their own authority and material or immaterial resources; they are of all shapes and sizes and sorts of social solidarity; some have grown spontaneously into full-fledged communities out of genealogical or territorial bonds while others were intentionally created to meet some collective need; but each of them is not only the creative source of institutions and rules of behavior proper to it but at the same time responsible for maintaining them by means of all sorts of corrective action.

For van Vollenhoven and his followers it was clear that the social scientific study of law, particularly if it is to be capable of taking account of, describing and analyzing the pluralism characteristic of social and legal systems, has to approach law as an attribute of social structure. Van Vollenhoven formulated as early as 1901 a conception of the social locus of law strikingly similar to that of the best modern descriptive theory of legal pluralism: Moore's conception of the "semi-autonomous social field" which "has rule-making capacities, and the means to induce or coerce compliance ... but ... is simultaneously set in a larger matrix which can, and does, affect and invade it, sometimes at the invitation of persons inside it, sometimes at its own instance" (Moore, 1973: 720).[5] The adat-law school produced forty years of solid scholarship in which the social locus of law was seen in *rechtsgemeenschappen*. Of all this work, the central and inspiring classic is van Vollenhoven's monumental *Adat-Law of the Dutch East Indies* (1918, 1931, 1933).

Van Vollenhoven was emphatically and universalistic in his ambitions. From the outset he recognized the importance of developing a set of technical concepts for the scientific study of law and of avoiding the use of folk concepts, particularly those derivative from the legal ideology and conceptual structure of western law. Anticipating Bohannan (1957, 1969), he insisted that every legal system first be understood in its own terms and only then be subsumed under the analytic categories of a universal science of law. In *Misconceptions of Adat-Law* (1909) he discussed at length the ways in which a sound understanding of adat-law had been impeded by the assumption that western folk categories such as 'ownership' are universally applicable. Since in the case of the Dutch East Indies, as we have seen, this question was of direct practical as well as of scientific importance, the resulting systematic misunderstanding not only led to poor science but also brought much down-to-earth injustice in its wake.[6] The same theme was taken up by ter Haar in the twilight years of the adat-law school, in his *Adat-Law in Indonesia* (1939; English translation 1948). Chapter XIII, "Legal Terminology", sums up the lessons learned from a third of a century of

[5] The concept of a *rechtsgemeenschap* is somewhat narrower than that of a semi-autonomous social field, in that the latter is not limited to corporate, property-holding groups. Cf. K. von Benda-Beckmann (1984a: 144 n. 19).

[6] In addition to 'ownership' and associated concepts, van Vollenhoven emphasized the non-universality of such fundamental classificatory principles of western legal thought as the distinction between rights *in personam* and rights *in rem* (see Sonius, 1976: 37-42).

Dutch legal ethnography. Out of this practical experience with the problems of translation and analysis implicit in a universal comparative approach had come considerable sophistication concerning the interdependence of every system of law with the language in which it is expressed, and the resulting importance – and difficulty – of seeking to purge folk elements from one's scientific vocabulary.

In many respects, the work of van Vollenhoven and the adat-law school, looked at in retrospect, was terribly modern. It was not until after the war that English and American anthroplogy of law – which since then has come to dominate the field – discovered for itself many of the insights and concepts and approaches which had been commonplace in the Dutch adat-law tradition since the early years of the century. That the Dutch adat-law literature is of great originality and sophistication – indeed, one of the two or three most important intellectual traditions in the anthropology of law – is beyond question.[7] Nevertheless, its influence outside the Netherlands and Indonesia has been small. Partly this is because until very recently almost none of the Dutch work had been translated.[8] The major exception being ter Haar's *Adat Law in Indonesia* (1948). Hoebel, who knew the Dutch literature and participated in the translation of ter Haar, made little use of it in his own work and rather misrepresented the Dutch contribution in his well-known treatise on legal anthropology, *The Law of Primitive Man* (1954). His own adherence to the 'trouble case' approach to law led him to misinterpret the Dutch scholars' insistence that law does not only manifest itself in cases of conflict, as if this were the same as the idea that the study of law consists of collecting statements of abstract rules from informants.[9] Hoebel's lack of interest in theoretical and analytic matters also led him to ignore completely a number of important Dutch contributions (e.g., the concepts of a *rechtsgemeenschap* and of *preventieve rechtszorg*). Apart from Hoebel, only a few English and American anthropologists and sociologists

---

[7]   The witness of the few persons in a position to compare it with the now-dominant Anglo-American tradition is uniformly to this effect. See Holleman (1973: 585; 1981a: 29); F. von Benda-Beckmann (1981b: 298-299); Lev (1984).

[8]   Until recently only a tiny part of van Vollenhoven's *oeuvre* was available in languages other than dutch: e.g., *La Découverte du Droit Indonésien* (1933), *The study of Indonesisan customary law* (1981a), and "Families of language and families of law" (1921). Recently, some of the more important parts of van Vollenhoven's work have been edited and translated under the supervision of Holleman: see van Vollenhoven (1981).

[9]   See note 3 above.

of law appear to know anything about, or to have been in the last influenced by, the Dutch tradition.[10]

The long-awaited English translation of a selection of van Vollenhoven's writing on adat-law finally appeared in 1981 (van Vollehoven, 1981). Holleman, who ultimately bore the editorial responsibility for the project and saw it to completion, describes the intertwining of the project's remarkably tortured history with that of the twilight days of the adat-law school, whose successive post-war representatives saw the project as a debt of honor. Sonius provides an introduction to van Vollenhoven's life and work (a somewhat shortened version of Sonius, 1976). It is to be hoped that, with this publication, the true dimensions of the Dutch tradition within the early history of legal anthropology will receive some belated international recognition and, more important, that some of the conceptual contributions of that tradition will make their way into the common scientific heritage. (See Lev, 1984, and F. von Benda-Beckmann, 1984, for reviews.)[11]

Succession and change in the adat-law tradition

After the way, the independence of Indonesia isolated adat-law scholarship in the Netherlands from its natural source of data and inspiration. Rather than abandon such a rich heritage, however, the University of Leiden decided to broaden its base. Van Vollenhoven's chair was renamed "Folk law and legal development in non-western societies" and the first steps were

---

[10] See Lev (1965, 1972, 1984); cf. also Hooker (1975). Pospisil, who has done extensive research in New Guinea, appears nevertheless not to know the adat-law literature (see e.g. Pospisil, 1971).

[11] The continuing significance of van Vollenhoven's work was the subject of talks presented at a commemoration of the 100th anniversary of his birth. Framed by talks on his work on international law and constitutional law, it was his almost single-handed creation of the discipline of adat-law scholarship as a systematic, scientific enterprise which occupied center stage. J.F. Holleman (1975b) emphasized the scope of van Vollenhoven's work and its continuing relevance for questions of legal policy and F. and K. von Benda-Beckmann (1975) addressed themselves to the central weakness in van Vollenhoven's approach to law, as seen from the perspective of modern legal anthropological fieldwork: the fact that despite his insistence on the importance of describing adat-law with appropriate analytic concepts and not with folk concepts derived from western legal ideas, his concept of 'law' remained a folk concept. In categorizing all social phenomena as 'legal' or 'non-legal', the ethnographer necessarily imports characteristically western values and concerns. The von Benda-Beckmanns proposed that field reseach address itself not to 'law' as a distinct category of phenomena, but to normative conceptions in general and to the patterns of behavior to which they are applicable (see further note 19).

taken toward a geographic reorientation, with Africa as a new focus of interest.

Meanwhile, van den Steenhoven, on the staff of the Catholic University of Nijmegen since 1963 and professor of folk law and legal development in non-western societies since 1972, established the Institute for Folk Law in 1973. Although his own scholarly experience was among the Eskimo,[12] the Institute oriented itself largely toward Indonesia. From the outset in Nijmegen, the study of 'folk law' was conceived of as neither purely scientific – van den Steenhoven rejected, for this reason, the appellation 'legal anthropology'' as a description of its work – nor as simply a branch of positive legal scholarship (despite some verbal adherence to ter Haar's *beslissingenleer*). Rather, what van den Steenhoven had in mind was empirical work carried out in the context of a specific moral commitment[13] and intended to be of a practical use to judges and other officials, who were presumed to be dedicated to the same general legal ideals or capable of being converted thereto by careful legal/empirical scholarship.

The other half of the adat-law heritage remained in Leiden. After a lapse of four years, J.F. Holleman was appointed in 1969 to the chair in Folk Law. He was unlike his predecessors in a number of respects. He had anthropological as well as legal training, his career had been largely devoted to field research, and his work had been in Southern Africa rather than Indonesia. Holleman thus combined in his person, as it were, a number of elements which defined the intellectual stage for anthropology of law in the Netherlands in the 1970s, in particular the convergence of the Dutch adat-law tradition with that of Anglo-American legal anthropology. His public lecture on his retirement in 1980, 'Folk Law at Leiden' (1981a), describes the history of the study of folk law at Leiden from the beginnings with van Vollenhoven through the period after the war in which the focus shifted to – or at least, was enlarged to include – Africa, the subject gradually came to identify itself self-consciously as social-scientific rather than juridical in nature, and the perspective changed from the top-down approach of

---

[12]   A full bibliography is to be found in Remie and Strijbosch (1981: 271-275).

[13]   Holleman's characterization of van Vollenhoven's fundamental moral commitment captures van den Steenhoven's as well (Holleman, 1981a: 18, quoting van Asbeck):

> The unity of all peoples in a world protected by a forceful, impartial legal order, in which the value and significance of all peoples receive appropriate recognition, and human potentialities, in all their variety, have an equal opportunity for full realization.

scholars who identified themselves with problems of administrations of colonial legal policy to a bottom-up perspective in which 'legal life on the ground floor' (1981a: 26, citing van Vollenhoven) is the central concern.

Since the war, the main new influence on the development of Dutch legal anthropology has come from outside, and specifically from Anglo-American legal anthropology in the persons of writers such as Gluckman (1973), Gulliver ;(1963, 1979), Hoebel (1954) and S.F. Moore (1978). They have heavily influenced the theoretical agenda and provided the models of fieldwork for the new generation of Dutch legal anthropologists. The result is a unique school of legal anthropology in which two major traditions – the adat-law tradition and the Anglo-American tradition – have been merged. If it looked for a while as if the adat-law tradition would go the way of German ethnological jurisprudence (Schott, 1982) and die without leaving much of an intellectual trace, the 1970s saw the beginnings of a rebirth of Dutch legal anthropology. Its intellectual vitality in the past decade gives reason for hope that Dutch legal anthropology will neither vanish altogether nor – what would be almost as great a shame – share the fate of Dutch sociology of law and be content to be little more than the bland and mediocre local variant of an international intellectual tradition whose roots and exciting developments are to be found elsewhere.

The 1970s

Institutional developments

As we have just seen, legal anthropology had an institutional base in two Dutch universities at the beginning of the 1970s: at the Catholic University of Nijmegen, where van den Steenhoven held the professorship in Folk Law and headed the Institute for Folk Law, dedicated to carrying on the adat-law tradition under changed circumstances, and at Leiden, where J.F. Holleman occupied the chair descended from van Vollenhoven. It is important to note that such institutionalization as there was, was within two *law* faculties. In fact, this has been true since the beginning of adat-law studies in the Netherlands. Not only the professorhips, but most research and teaching of anthropology of law took place, and to this day takes place, in law faculties. Dutch anthropology as a discipline has never shown much interest in the anthropology of law, being willing at best to provide a joint appointment for a legal anthropologist (as in the cases of Holleman and van den Steenhoven).

The only important exceptions to that generalization are the Law Section in the African Studies Center and the chair in non-western agrarian law at the Agricultural University of Wageningen. In 1967, when J.F. Holleman was head of the African Studies Center, Emile van Rouveroy van Nieuwaal, a legal anthropologist, was appointed to its staff. The intention was to undertake a major program of research in African law. During the rest of the 1970s the Law Section organized a number of international symposia, carried out an active research program, produced a number of interestinig publications and films, and in general came to occupy an important place among the handful of institutional locations where anthropology of law is practised in the Netherlands.[14] In 1982 F. von Benda-Beckmann was appointed to the existing but long-vacant chair in non-western agrarian law at the Agricultural University of Wageningen, and the focus of the chair was enlarged to include an emphasis on indigenous and local law as well as national legislation and the like.

After the retirement of van den Steenhoven in 1981, F. Strijbosch was appointed Director of the Institute for Folk Law. Its continuing importance as an institutional base for Dutch anthropology of law was thereby assured.

The 1970s saw one profound institutional loss for Dutch legal anthropology: the abandonment of van Vollenhoven's chair in Leiden. After the retirement of J.F. Holleman, the law faculty of Leiden University decided not to maintain the chair in folk law and non-western legal development. As Holleman observed at the time, the spectacle was a shameful one. Leiden simply

> abandoned a field in which she had once held the leading position internationally and thereafter always a highly respected one; (Leiden will now also) have to give up the pretense of offering a well-rounded study program providing insight into the most important material and immaterial problems of non-western societies. Because that will simply not be true! (1981a: 29)

---

[14] Because of internal reorganizations within the Africa Studies Center, the future of the Law Section, and hence of an institutional base for research in anthropology of law, is at present uncertain.

116

Against this profound institutional loss at Leiden one small optimistic note can be set: the Law Faculty there has recently re-established the part-time, externally-financed chair in African constitutional law. The job-description emphasizes the importance of local 'customary' constitutional systems to the study of the constitutional law of African states, and the consequent importance of approaching the subject from an anthropological as well as a legal perspective. Emile van Rouveroy van Nieuwaal of the Law Section of the African Studies Centre has been appointed to this professorship.

Two institutional fruits of van den Steenhoven's organisational and catalyzing gifts require mention here. In 1976 he organized the *Volksrechtkring* (Folk Law Group), whose annual sessions have afforded a regular opportunity for all those directly or indirectly involved in legal anthropology to get together for extended discussions of matters of common concern and whose *Newsletter* from 1976 onwards provided an essential medium of communication in the small but growing and changing world of Dutch legal anthropology. The collective labors of the *Volksrechtkring* have so far been devoted to a common publication project: *Issues in Folk Law and Legal Pluralism* (forthcoming), consisting largely of original essays on work – theoretical and empirical – being done by Dutch legal anthropologists. By the end of the 1970s the *Volksrechtkring* had over 30 members, including everyone in the Netherlands who is actively engaged in legal anthropology.

Toward the end of the 1970s van den Steenhoven recapitulated the history of the *Volksrechtkring* on a world scale. Again working with the Institute in Nijmegen as an organizational base, he put together the Commission on Folk Law and Legal Pluralism, a working commission of the International Union of Anthropological and Ethnographic Sciences. During the start-up phase, from 1978 to 1981, the Commission was almost entirely a creature of the Institute and of van den Steenhoven's organizational energy. A *Newsletter*, edited (by F. Strijbosch) and published in Nijmegen, was distributed to a worldwide membership which quickly grew to over 125 members, distributed over 35 countries in all continents. The results of the Commission's first scientific conference, "State institutions and their use of folk law", held in Bellagio in September, 1981, will shortly be published (Allott and Woodman, 1985).

Finally, the end of the 1970s saw an important shift in the institutional relationship between anthropology and sociology of law, a development which promises to be of great importance in the coming years. When, in 1980, an informal association of Dutch and Flemish sociologists of law who had gathered annually for a number of years decided to found a professional association, the Association for the Social-Scientific Study of Law, the decision was taken to try to bridge the artificial boundary which had until then tended to keep sociologists and anthropologists of law relatively isolated from one another. The success of this initiative led quickly to a number of related moves, among them the merging of the *Newsletter* of the *Volksrechtkring* with *NNR*, the organ of the Association. In the same spirit, the Working Group (*werkgemeenschap*) set up on the initiative of the Association as the first stage in the selection of research proposals for funding by the national Foundation for Pure Scientific Research (ZWO) includes anthropologists as well as sociologists of law (together with criminologists and psychologists). These institutional development in the direction of breaking down the historically-accidental division between anthropology and sociology of law have had their parallel on the personal side, and in particular in the fact that the small group of practitioners of sociology of law now includes several with some exposure to and affinity for the anthropological tradition. As we will see later on in this trend report (§2.3.3), the increased exposure of the two traditions to each other is now beginning to bear fruit in research.

Personal developments

At the outset of the 1970s, the only two representative of Dutch legal anthropology actively on the scene were J.F. Holleman and van den Steenhoven. By the early 1980s, both had retired. In the meantime they had striven successfully to keep the adat-law tradition alive, to publicize it, and to pass it along to a new generation – Holleman largely through his writings and van den Steenhoven largelyl through his organizational activities. H. Sonius should also be mentioned in this connection. A student of van Vollenhoven's, he worked for almost a quarter of a century in the colonial administration of the Dutch East Indies, and thereafter carried out research concerning African land law as a member of the staff of the African Studies Center (1959-1967). In recent years, he has published an intellectual biography of van Vollenhoven (1976) and a study of local administration

118

and land law in the Dutch East Indies (1980).

In the course of the decade, a number of new faces were added. The most prominent members of this new generation so far are:[15]

Frans von Benda-Beckmann (born 1941 in Griefswald, Germany): since 1982 professor of agrarian law of non-western societies at the Agricultural University of Wageningen; from 1978 to 1982, director of the Netherlands Research Center for the Law of South-East Asia and the Caribbean in Leiden.[16] He received his legal training at the University of Kiel (Dr. jur. 1970). During 1967-1968 he did legal research in Zambia and Malawi which resulted in a dissertation, *Rechtspluralism in Malawi* (1970). From 1972 to 1977 he was on the staff of the Ethnological Seminar of the University of Zürich and a lecturer in legal anthropology; during 1974-75 he did field research (together with his wife, K. von Benda-Beckmann) in West Sumatra, the results of which were published as *Property in Social Continuity* (1979a), on the basis of which he received his Habilitation. Since 1979 he has been Privatdozent for Ethnology at the University of Zürich. He is the author of numerous articles on African and Indonesian law and legal pluralism, and on various theoretical and methodological problems of legal anthropology. In 1981 he organized the conference on "Law and Development" held at Leiden University. Since 1981 he has been an Associate Editor of the *Journal of Legal Pluralism*. He is a member of the Executive Body of the Commission on Folk Law and Legal Pluralism.

K. von Benda-Beckmann (born 1946 in The Hague): since 1982 part-time lecturer on the law faculty of the Erasmus University, Rotterdam. She received her law degree from the University of Amsterdam in 1972. She is the author of several articles on law in Indonesia and in Minangkabau in particuuar. Her dissertation, *The Broken Stairways to Consensus: Village Justice and State Courts in Minangkabau* (Catholic University of Nijmegen,

---

[15] There are of course many others whose writings occasionally or incidentally have points of contact with legal anthropology. Among anthropologists, the recent writings of Kuper (1970a, 1970b, 1971) are of special interest. Goldschmidt's dissertation, *National and Indigenous Constitutional Law in Ghana: Their development and Their Relation to Each Other* (Law Faculty, Leiden University, 1981) makes extensive use of the anthropological literature. Lette (1981) and den Ouden (1981) make interesting ethnographic contributions. (See also note 26).

[16] The Center and its history are briefly described in Bakri-Sigit and F. von Benda – Beckmann (1981).

1984), based on the fieldwork which she carried out together with her husband F. von Benda-Beckmann, has recently been published.

Emile van Rouveroy van Nieuwaal (born in Eindhoven in 1939): since 1967 senior research officer, Law Section, Africa Studies Center, Leiden University; recently appointed to the chair in African constitutional law at the University of Leiden. He received his law degree from the University of Groningen in 1967. During 1969-71 he carried out field research (together with his wife, Els van Rouveroy van Nieuwaal) in Northern Togo; his dissertation at the Law Faculty of the University of Leiden (1976) was based on this research and appeared in book form in French in 1977 under the title *A la Recherche de la Justice – Quelques Aspects du Droit Matrimonial et de la Justice du Juge de Paix et du Chef Supérieur des Anufòm à Mango dans le Nord du Togo*. He has regularly returned to Northern Togo for further research, in particular in 1977-78. In addition to several activities on Anufò and Togolese law – and especially on their interaction – he and his wife have made a number of films deriving from their field work in Togo. In 1978 he organized an international congress on "La réforme agro-foncière dans les pays du Conseil de l'Entente" in Lama-Kara, Togo, and in 1980 one on "Le documentaire socio-scientifique en Afrique francophone" in Amsterdam. He is a member of the Editorial Advisory Board of the *Journal of Legal Pluralism*.

Els van Rouveroy van Nieuwaal-Baerends (born in 1943 in the Hague) has recently been appointed part-time lecturer in sociology of law at the University of Groningen (with special responsibility for anthropology of law). She received her degree in anthropology at the University of Groningen in 1968 and has lectured there in anthropology from time to time. She carried out field work in Northern Togo together with her husband Emile van Rouveroy van Nieuwaal, resulting in several joint articles and films, and providing the data for the dissertation on which she is currently working.

M.K. Slaats-Portier (born 1948 in Surabaya), associated since 1976 with the Institute for Folk Law in Nijmegen. She received her degree in anthropology from the Catholic University of Nijmegen in 1973. Her field work was carried out in Northern Sumatra together with her husband H. Slaats, resulting in a joint dissertation in 1981 – *Rights in Land and their*

Realization in karo Batak Society (Law Faculty, Catholic University of Nijmegen).

H. Slaats (born 1943 in Waalwijk) has also been associated with the Institute of Folk Law since 1976. He received his degree in law from the Catholic University of Nijmegen in 1972. In addition to their dissertation, he and his wife have written several articles deriving from their research in Karoland.

A Strijbosch (born 1943, Nijmegen): since 1970 a member of the staff of the Institute for Folk Law of the Catholic University of Nijmegen and its director since 1983. He received his law degree in 1970 from the Catholic University of Nijmegen. During 1971-1973 he was carried out field reseach concerning the adat-law of Lombok. His dissertation, *Lawyers and the Study of Folk Law in the Dutch East Indies and Anglophone Africa* (Law Faculty, Catholic Univeristy of Nijmegen) was published in 1980. He has written several articles deriving from his Lombok research and on other subjects. Since the retirement of van den Steenhoven, he is the coordinator of the *Volksrechtkring* and the editor of its section of *NNR*. He is also responsible for the secretariat of the Commission on Folk Law and Legal Pluralism, a member of its Executive Body, and editor of its *Newsletter*, as well as a member of the Editorial Advisory Board of the *Journal of Legal Pluralism*. He is a member of the executive committee of the Association for the Social-Scientific Study of Law.

Two others, themselves not practicing anthropologists of law but active participants in recent developments, should be briefly noted:

G. van den Bergh, professor of legal history at the University of Utrecht and principal author, among numerous other writings, of *Staphorst en Zijn Gerichten, Staphorst and its Village Tribunals* (1980). He was chairman of the Dutch project-advisory committee of the Bali-Lombok Project. He is a member of the Editorial Advisory Board of the *Journal of Legal Pluralism*.

J. Griffiths, professor of sociology of law at the University of Groningen since 1977. He is a member of the Executive Body of the Commission on Folk Law and Legal Pluralism. He played a leading role in setting up the Association for the Social-Scientific Study of Law and opening its membership to anthropologists (and psychologists) as well as sociologists of law, and was until recently a member of its executive committee. Since 1979 he has been the Editor-in-Chief of the *Journal of Legal Pluralism*.

Research in the 1970s

Dutch research within the tradition of legal anthropology has addressed a wide variety of problems in a number of different societies during the last decade. The survey which follows adopts a simple geographical organizational principle, one which more or less corresponds to the historical development of the field in the Netherlands. We begin with Indonesia, consider next Africa, and finish with research in the Netherlands itself.

Indonesia

Bali-Lombok

The Bali-Lombok Project was the largest and most ambitous legal anthropological research project since the war and the first major undertaking of the newly-established Institute for Folk Law in Nijmegen. The aim of the project was twofold: a) To investigate the locl adat law of Bali and Lombok and to put the resulting findings "at the disposal of the courts, the lawyers and other law-seekers in these regions ... (and) those charged with the task of developing and forming national law ...." (Koesnoe, 1977: 12); b) To serve as an experiment in interdisciplinary and international cooperative research. The history of the project and a discussion of some of its results has been provided by Koesnoe (1977). As a rare example of a full and detailed account of a complete research project, this is a revealing and useful document. In many respects the project was a failure, and the reasons for this lay not in insufficient investment of time and energy nor in inadequate planning. The problem lay in scientific and organizational naiveté on a number of critical dimensions, in particular with respect to the demands and limitations of interdisciplinary and intercultural research.

Despite lavish investments the project proved fairly barren. With the exception of two papers by Strijbosch it has as far produced no published findings. In "Credit transactions on the Island of Lombok" (1981a) Strijbosch describes the more or less standardized forms of loan agreements (generally with security and very high interest) used on Lombok, the social processes by which they are arrived at, and the social consequences of such transactions (gradual redistribution of the pledged land from small, local farmers to a wealthier group of Balinese landholders and Javanese military and commercial figures). In his contribution to the Bellagio symposium of the Commission on Folk Law and Legal Pluralism, "Recognition of folk institutions for dispute settlement in Lombok, Indonesia" (1981b), he describes the official and non-official institutions available to villagers with conflicts, as these functioned in the early 1970s after de-recognition of the unofficial institutions by the state. In fact, disputes generally came before village institutions before being taken to state courts, but there was no cooperation between the two sets of institutions. Strijbosch concludes by observing that recognition would entail resolving some difficult technical problems (identification of the recognized institutions; definition of their jurisdiction). With the exception of Strijbosch' work, the Bali-Lombok project has remained barren so far.

Karo-land

In 1969 van den Steenhoven conducted a brief stint of field research in Karo-land, in North Sumatra, and collected a number of cases of *runggun adat*, the Karo institution of collective decision-making (used among other things in cases of dispute). He analyzed the social and ideological context of this kind of decision-making-by-consensus in his article, "Musjawarah in Karo-land" (1973; see also van den Steenhoven, 1970).

Between 1973 and 1978 H. Slaats and K. Slaats-Portier carried out field research during three periods totalling more than two and a half years. In *Land Rights and their Realization in Karo Batak Society* (1981a; see also 1981b) they describe the social organization and kinship system of the Karo Batak, the system of relationships to land, the allocation of land rights, and the institution of *runggun adat*. A second volume contains the full text of three cases of *runggun*, translated (into Dutch) and annotated. It makes a thoroughly-researched and carefully-described contribution to the ethnographic literature on situations in which authority is largely absent, compromise solutions are the usual and expected outcome, and decision takes place by mutual agreement. The contribution could, however, have been greater had they taken more explicit account of relevant theory: as it is, Karo Batak society, and especially its legal dimension, are presented as idosyncratic and isolated.[17]

Slaats and Slaats-Portier have recently returned to the field and are currently working on the relationship between economic change and change in local adat.

Minangkabau

In 1974-1975 F. von Benda-Beckmann and K. von Benda-Beckmann carried out field research for some 14 months in Minangkabau. They were concerned with the following subjects: the social-political organization of the Minangkabau *nagari* (historically more or less autonomous village republics), the processes of dispute settlement in *nagari* institutions and in the state courts (K. von Benda-Beckmann), and the system of property relationships and inheritance (F. von Benda-Beckmann).[18]

This research project has led to a number of publications. F. von Benda-Beckmann's *Property in Social Contuinity: Continuity and Change in the Maintenance of Property Relationships through Time in Minangkabau, West Sumatra* (1979a) deals with the historical development of Minangkabau concepts, rules and institutions concerning property relationships and inheritance, and with the associated behavior. The description and analysis of a particular legal institution and its use is set in the context of the legal pluralism characteristic of Indonesian society, and of the changing political, social and economic circumstances of Minangkabau. The first virtue of the book is as a detailed and careful ethnography focussed upon a central legal institution, and as such it is an important contribution to the literature of legal anthropology. Von Benda-Beckmann's ambitions are more than ethnographic, however. He aims to further the development of anthropological theory in relation to the concepts of law, property and inheritance, and to illustrate a particular methodological approach to the study of legal norms and institutions. Social organization in general, he argues, can be seen in functional terms as the

---

[17] Compare the review by K. von Benda-Beckmann (1982b).

[18] In K. and F. von Benda-Beckmann (1981a) they give a nice account of some of the problems they encountered in securing information concerning adat-law and village conflicts from local informants.

"relative degree to which the autonomy of society's members is recognized and restricted." It "mediates between the self-interest of society's members and the interest of the community" (1979as: 18). Such limitation of individual autonomy generally takes place by means of social institutions which "lay down generalized channels of problem-solution in terms of cognitive and normative conceptions" (1979a: 19). Law can best be seen for empirical purposes as an aspect of every such social isntitution: it "consists in the objectified cognitive and normative conceptions by means of which society recognizes and restricts its members' autonomy to act and to construct their own cognitive and normative conceptions" (1979a: 28). In the course of his discussion von Benda-Beckmann effectively disposes of a variety of existing conceptions of law prevalent among legal anthropologists, such as those which "relegate law to (one) domain of social organization" (the "casuistic" approach) or which "reserve law for those forms of normative conceptions which are peculiar to a specific form of political organizatin (such as the state)" (the "typological" approach). He observes that if one restricts the concept of law to "objectified conceptions" – rules, and the concepts used in them – this does not mean that the social processes in which rules play a part are to be ignored. But "(objectified) conceptions should not be confused with the social processes in which they are produced and manipulated, nor with the referents which serve as their legitimation, such as the will of the people, the command of the sovereign, traditional behavior patterns, etc." (1979a: 39).[19]

In short, von Benda-Beckmann has dealt with the problem of an empirical concept of law in an original, powerful and refined way, which takes account of most of the difficulties which legal anthropologists have had with the concept over the last half century. In his discussion of the concepts of

---

[19]   In a joint article preparatory to their fieldwork (see also note 11), the von Benda – Beckmanns explored the inadequacies of existing concepts of law as an empirical category. They came to the conclusion that –

> What we want to investigate is, on the one hand, the social sphere of the products of normative thinking, which in Indonesia is differentiated by a pluralism of normative systems and a pluralism of procedures which bring forth and apply the products of normative thinking. On the other hand, we want to investigate the behavioral processes to which this normative material applies, and the mutual relationships between the two spheres. (K. and F. von Benda-Beckmann, 1975: 20).

property and inheritance, too, von Benda-Beckmann makes a significant contribution to the theoretical literature.

Finally, von Benda-Beckmann's book is an important application of a particular methodological approach to the study of law. "Law and legal institutions are ... analyzed simultaneously from a long-term historical perspective and from the perspective of individual-centered, short-term, choice-making instrumental action and interaction" (1979a: 6, quoting Moore, 1970: 294). Law is seen in terms both of rules and conceptions and of the actual behavior of individuals and of officials to which those rules and conceptions apply. Von Benda-Beckmann argues from the literature for the necessity of combining an historical, macro- with a synchronic, micro-perspective, and of attending to both norms and practice, and he abundantly illustrates this argument with the quality of the data and the persuasiveness of the analysis which such methodological principles make possible.

Property in Social Continuity is in my opinion clearly the most important Dutch contribution to the anthropology of law – and, for that matter, to the more inclusive field of sociology of law generally – in the period under review here. By comparison with other work by Dutch anthropologists of law during the 1970s it excels in the scope of its scientific ambitions, in the quality of its data, and in the sharpness and sophisticiation of its analysis. It will without doubt come to rank among the important anthropological studies of a legal institution. In this connection the fact that von Benda-Beckmann published in English is of critical importance. It has given his work, by contrast with that of some other Dutch anthropologists and of most Dutch sociologists of law, access to the international scientific forum.[20]

K. von Benda-Beckmann has put the phenomenon of legal pluralism at the center of her analysis in a series of articles, several of which have since

[20] *Property in Social Continuity* has been widely and enthusiastically reviewed in international scientific journals. Particularly interesting are: Roberts in the *Modern Law Review* (1983), where the book is adjudged "an important contribution to (the) enterprise (of putting the study of rules and of action back together again)", but a protest is entered against the failure to give any content to the idea of the 'legal' within the totality of social control; Kahn in *Indonesia Circle* (1980), describing the book as providing "far and away the best material on Minangkabau *adat* from a local level that is available to us at the present time" but taking issue with a number of specific arguments (especially with regard to the analysis of legal and social change); and S.F. Moore in the *Journal of Legal Pluralism* (1983), observing that "as a discussion of Minangkabau concepts of social organization and property (the) book is a significant contribution to the field of legal anthropology" (1983: 165).

been published in her dissertation, *The Broken Stairways to Consensus: Village Justice and State Courts in Minangkabau* (1984). In "Forum shopping and shopping forums" (1981a) she describes the variety of institutions available for dispute processing in the pluralistic setting of a Minangkabau village and the nature of their pluralistic setting of a Minankabau village and the nature of their competitive relationships with each other. She focusses on the forum-shopping behavior of individuals and the corresponding behavior of institutions which compete with each other for legal business, illustrating her general argument with a very full description of a complicated case. A noteworthy aspect of her analysis is the attention she gives to the way in which the socio-political structure of the village is reflected in legal argument. During the forum-selection stage of a dispute in Minangkabau, the pluralistic social context dominates in legal argument, which tends to revolve around jurisdictional issues. Once an institution has assumed jurisdiction, legal argument addresses almost exclusively question of the procedural implications of social structural relationships: "everything that happens land has happened; in the case is evaluated in terms of procedural norms" – that is to say, norms governing the conduct of public affairs and regulating the political and status relationships of the participants (1981a: 145).

In several more recent articles she takes the theme of legal reasoning in its social context and as a part of social processes several steps further. She seeks to show how the different results reached with adat norms in state courts from what one would expect in local institutions can be accounted for. The stage is set for "systematic misunderstanding" (Bohannon 1965: 39) by the far greater differentiation of state law, and especially its distinction between substantive and procedural rules. Since much of adat law concerns not so much *what* is to be done as *how* it is to be done, and indigenous legal argument is therefore strongly "procedural" in orientation, the application of the western distinction and the reception of adat substantive rules only, means that the adat-law applied in state courts is a truncated and for villagers almost unrecognizable travesty of their law.

In a pair of articles K. von Benda-Beckmann discusses the difference in style of legal reasoning (systematic breaking-down of a case into its component elements vrs. holistic treatment of all components as inseparably interrelated) at the various stages of a proceeding from formulation of the issue through execution of the judgment, and the reception of evidence and its assessment for relevance and reliability (K. von Benda-Beckmann, 1981c and 1985; see also 1982a). In the latter article she shows, among other things, how western objections to hearsay and opinion evidence and to witnesses who are too closely related to the parties clash with the local conception that adat functionaries and others involved in processes of 'preventive law care' are the most reliable of all sources of information. In both articles she emphasizes the different meaning of a 'decision' in the two legal orders: for the state courts, the only relevant decision is the judgment, whereas the villagers, used to processes in which an entire dispute is treated and disposed of as a whole, tend to assume that the winning party has been found in the right not only on the narrow question decided (e.g., a possessory claim to a piece of land) but also with respect to the underlying dispute of which that immediate issue may have been a superficial incident (e.g., a question of lineage membership, with implications both for future inheritance and for political relationships). A decision taken on burden-of-proof grounds with respect to a minor and derivative issue may therefore be interpreted locally as a decision on the merits of far larger matters.

Her most recent article, "The social significance of Minangkabau state court decisions" (1984b), deals with the execution phase of dispute settlement in court. She shows that the actual results of a decision are often not at all the same as what the decision contemplates, that a decision does not determine its social consequences but becomes one among many relevant factors in the social field of the parties. The 'extended case method', in other words, must be extended to include what happens *after* a dispute is 'settled'.

In a joint article (1981b) the von Benda-Beckmanns discuss the problems involved in studying changes in local law over time, using the historical development of the Minangkabau matrilinear social organization and inheritance system as an example. The imminent collapse of this system was predicted by Dutch scholars as long ago as the 1920s and its actual collapse has been reported from time to time ever since. The fact is, however, that there is no indication of its actual or impending demise. The shifts that have taken place have been gradual rather than dramatic, and amount to adjustments within the matrilinear system rather than its abandonment. The von Benda-Beckmanns show convincingly that three key ethnological mistakes are responsible for such profound misunderstanding of what is going on. In the first place, Dutch scholars have made constant use of the folk concepts of Dutch law in analyzing Minangkabau legal phenomena.

Forcing those phenomena (despite van Vollenhoven's warning on this very point) into the category of 'ownership' – either 'individual' or 'collective' and in either case essentially 'private' in character – and assuming a clear differentiation of 'law' and 'legal rights' from other social norms and rights, led these scholars to overestimate the collective element of 19th century Minangkabau property relationships and the individualistic elements in the present situation. In the second place, the alleged dramatic change rests on a false comparison, in which a change in one rule is seen in isolation from the structure of the relevant law as a whole, and an apparently collective aspect of 19th century adat law is compared with a more individual element in modern adat law. But if the entire legal situation in both periods is compared – not just that which fits within a conception of 'ownership' or 'inheritance' – the change seems much less profound. Finally, the predicted collapse of the matrilineal system assumes a rigid correlation between socio-economic development and legal change. The fact is, however, especially in an adat-law system which emphasizes the assessment of concrete situations and which consists more of procedural requirements than of commands and prohibitions, that profound adjustments to socio-economic change can and have taken place without entailing much change in the applicable rules of law. The von Benda-Beckmanns' conclusion is, then, that changes in practice have not been nearly so great as is generally assumed, and that the changes which have taken place have mostly been possible within the structure of existing law.[21]

Ambon

The von Benda-Beckmanns have recently returned to the field, this time to Ambon, for a study of the role of local and national law in the provision of social security.

---

[21]   F. von Benda-Beckmann deals with a number of the same ideas in two other articles: In "Ayam gadang toh batalua? Changing values in Minangkabau property and inheritance law and their relation to structural change" (1982a) he puts the emphasis on what *has* changed in Minangkabau law and social strucutre. In "The development of folk property laws in complex societies" (1982b) he again deals with the theme of legal change in Minangkabau, this time with special emphasis on the situation of legal pluralism.

A further article deriving from the Minangkabau research project (F. and K. von Benda-Beckmann, 1979) deals in a popular way with the tension between state and adat law in Indonesia since colonial times, and with the increasing centralism of national legal policy in Indonesia.

Africa

Rhodesia
In 1975 J.F. Holleman returned to Rhodesia for a brief period of fieldwork after absence of 25 years.[22] His attention was in particular directed to the tensions and conflicts built into the relationship between tribal and governmental jurisdiction. In "Disparities and uncertainties in African law and judicial authority: a Rhodesian case study" (1979a) he deals with the troubled relationship between tribal and governmental authority in Rhodesia (now Zimbabwe). Despite the hegemonic pretensions of the Rhodesian government, there had been for almost a century a dual system of authority with which the rural population had more or less learned to cope. But

> three quarters of a century of European political dominance and cultural enterprise (mainly in economics and education) ... had not only progressively undermined the traditional basis of tribal authority, but changed its very nature and function by imposing upon it a host of duties and responsibilities (as local agents of the central government) that are anything but traditional (1979a: 25).

The effort to decentralize administration by 'returning power to the chiefs' was thus bound to fail and to lead to profound confusion concerning the locus of local authority. Fail it did, and Holleman describes in detail one dramatic instance of the resulting collapse of the "tottering structure of law and authority" (1979a: 23).

In another article deriving from the same research Holleman focusses on litigation processes in the Rhodesian circumstances of profound and tense dualism (1979b). After describing the general situation and a number of

---

[22]   Holleman's earlier fieldwork in Rhodesia is treated in numerous publications, among them his authoritative work, *Shona Customary Law* (1952). *Cf.* also *Chief, Council and Commissioner – Some Problems of Government in Rhodesia* (1969). Other work in the 1970s includes Holleman (1974) and (1975a).

cases[23] he turns to the question, what sort of scholarship is capable of handling such a state of affairs? Research on law in circumstances of legal pluralism must break through the limitations of traditional legal and anthropological scholarship in two ways: by focussing on the *interaction* of the various spheres of legal order, and by focussing more on "non-litigious praxis" as an essential locus of law in society. But an adequate picture of law cannot be formed by a mere collage of legal research concerning the higher strata and anthropological research concerning the lower. A "closer partnership" is necessarily, in which each discipline, while retaining its own "disciplinary skills of perception and conception" also goes "as far as possible to adopt those of the other" (1979b: 130).

Togo
Since 1969, Emile and Els van Rouveroy van Nieuwaal have been carrying out research in northern Togo (1969-1971; 1971-1978). Since his formal training is in law and hers in anthropology, and the focus of their work together has been on the interaction between official and local law at the village level and the effects of this interaction on daily transactions as well as on the handling of dispute cases, their work can be seen as a practical realization in one setting of Holleman's program for research.

Emile van Rouveroy van Nieuwaal's dissertation was preceded by a number of articles deriving from this research in Togo, of which the two most important for our purposes[24] are:

– "To claim or not to claim: changing views about the restitution of marriage prestations among the Anufòm of Northern Togo" (E. & E. van Rouveroy van Nieuwaal, 1975b), in which the Anufò system of reciprocal exchanges of marriageable women between patrilineages is described, and the consequences of its inconsistency with the provisions of official Togolese (that is, French) marriage law for the relationships between the local judicial representatives of the two legal order is analyzed. Among its other virtues, this article is one of the few places in the ethnographic literature in which the tendency of the substantive law applied by competing tribunals to

---

[23] One of these cases, involving conflicting Shona and Western notions concerning the permissible presumptions applicable to the problem of 'proving' a homicide, is more fully described, and the conflicts and misunderstandings produced by the dualistic tension of the Rhodesian situation further discussed, in Holleman (1981b).

[24] For reference to some earlier articles see Emile van Rouveroy van Nieuwaal (1977a: 265-266).

converge (cf. Griffiths, 1981b) is described in detail.

– "The plot of the sophisticated son-in-law" (Emile van Rouveroy van Nieuwaal, 1975b), dealing with another sort of tension between the two legal orders: that arising out of their inconsistent provisions for establishing rights in land. The possibilities for more or less unscrupulous manipulation which the superposition of 'modern' land law in such a context office, especially to those with better access to information and power, are illustrated with a case-history.

The dissertation itself, *A la Recherche de la Justice* (1977a), describes the historical development of legal pluralism in Togo, the history and social structure of Anufò society and the structure of its adjudicatory system (which, although it is not recognized as such by the Togolese state, in fact disposes of far more judicial business than the local official court). Against this background, the focus is upon the interaction of the two systems and the possibilities such interaction gives to litigants to engage in 'forum shopping'. Special attention is paid to factors which may affet litigant choice, such as: the lower costs of the official court and its ability to enforce its judgments with police force if necessary; the ability of the chief's court to dispose of cases in a way which does a minimum of violence to ongoing social relationships; the differences in substantive law (the law applied in the state court is, for instance, more favorable to the autonomy of women); the involvement of the Chief in local political relationships (which, of course, can cut both ways); etc. As in the earlier article, "To claim or not to claim ...", the tendency of the two bodies of substantive law to converge under the pressure of their competitive relationship is emphasized. These general themes are illustrated with eight extensive case histories involving litigation in one or the other court or both, and in which the proceedings were directly observed. The strength of the book lies in its account of the Anufò social system, their matrimonial law, and its application and change in circumstances of legal pluralism. Its weakness lies in its failure fully to exploit the opportunity to put its subject in the larger perspective of comparable ethnographic literature and relevant theory. (Van Rouveroy van Nieuwaal's dissertation is reviewed in Griffiths, 1977.)

More recently the van Rouveroy van Nieuwaals have returned to their data from northern Togo. In "Possibilities and impossibilities of conciliation among the Anufòm in Northern Togo" (1981b), they discuss the social preconditions of successful conciliation and show that these are present in the case of the Chief's court but not in that of the state court. The ultimate object of their analysis is to contribute to the development of a comparative study of conciliation.[25]

Els van Rouveroy van Nieuwaal is currently preparing a dissertation concerning the semi-permanent debt relationships entailed by the Anufò system of exchange of marriageable women between patrilineages, and the consequences which these relationships have for social and economic organization (including dispute-processing) in general, and for the position of women in particular.

The van Rouveroy van Nieuwaals are unique among Dutch anthropologists of law – and belong to a very select international company – in that they have presented their findings not only via the printed word but also in the form of ethnographic films. Their research in Northern Togo had led to four films dealing with dispute processing in the circumstances described and analyzed in their writings: *Mbambim* (1973) concerns the handling of disputes at the level of the lineage (including the role of soothsaying): *Bekoindintu* (1980) shows how a single conflict can be the subject of repeated handling by a village headman: *Sherea* (1975a) shows the operation of the court of the Chief; and *In Search of Justice* (1981a) compares the way in which disputes are handled at the various levels of the local system with adjudication in the lowest court of the Togolese state. In addition, *A Toad in the Courtyard* (1979) illustrates the difficult and unstable constitutional position of a Chief, who must balance between his responsibility toward his own society and the responsibility imposed on him by the state; the film consists largely of an extensive interview with the Chief of the Anufò shortly after his deposition by the Togolese government.

Both the cinematographic quality and the ethnological sophistication of these films has strikingly improved over the last decade. *In Search of Justice* is in both respects a major contribution to the international common property of such films. One of the most interesting resources presently at the

[25] Other articles deriving from the research in Togo include Emile van Rouveroy van Nieuwaal (1975a, 1977b, 1979, 1980a and 1980b), and Emile and Els van Rouveroy van Nieuwaal (1976).

disposal of Dutch anthropology and sociology of law is a growing experience with ethnographic filming.[26]

Ongoing research in Africa

Ab van Eldijk of the Department of Non-western Law of the Agricultural University, Wageningen, is conducting field research in Sierra Leone concerning the organization of the trade in and transportation of agricultural produce from the farmers in the hinterland to the markets in Freetown. The central focus will be upon the legal aspect of this organization – the various systems of applicable norms and their interaction, the actual use of the options made available by the various norms as the actors seek to achieve predictability and security, and the prevention, regulation and processing of conflict.

In Senegal the African Studies Center is currently engaged in a major study of land tenure. The focus of this research is on the interaction between local and national law with respects to land rights and land use. It is being carried out by G. Hesseling, a lawyer, whose dissertation (1982) is a legal/political study of the reception of French constitutional law in Senegal, and by M. Sypkens Smit, an anthropologist.[27]

---

[26]   Apart from the extensive research in Togo, the African Studies Center mounted one other large research project concerning law in Africa during the 1970s: the Sierra Leone project on developments in family law. Its results were quite disappointing, especially insofar as the legal anthropological side of the project is concerned (see Harrell-Bond, 1975; Harrell-Bond and Rijnsdorp, 1975, 1977; Rijnsdorp, 1975). Other, incidental contributions of staff-members of the African Studies Center include van Binsbergen (1977) and Konings (1984). Roberts (1977) contains the proceedings of a conference on law and the family in Africa, including several of the articles mentioned above as well as E. & E. van Rouveroy van Nieuwaal 1975b).

[27]   Cf. Klei and Hesseling (197). Sypkens Smit had earlier, as a student, carried out research into patterns of access to rice-land in the Basse-Casamance area of Senegal. His research took place in the context of a larger study by the African Studies Center into the causes of migration in southwest Senegal. Scarcity of rice-land due to unequal distribution had been suggested as an explanation, but the redistributive 'lending' mechanism available within the local property/kinship system appeared to deprive such an explanation of much of its force. Sypkens Smit's research problem was to analyze this latter argument by means of a quantitative study of the redistributive effects of the lending mechanism. He concludes (1976) that the land-loan system seems to be so profoundly rectifying any inequality in the distribution of land resulting from the inheritance system that scarcity could hardly be a significant cause of migration. The study as such is a small methodological jewel. The practical working of the inheritance and land-loan norms of local law is made manifest and concrete by the simple expedient of enquiring into the provenance of every plot being farmed by a given group of farmers.

The Netherlands

The only substantial legal anthropological research project carried out in the Netherlands itself deals with the village tribunals (*volksgerichten*) of a rural farming community, Staphorst (van den Bergh and others, 1980). The project entailed a variety of sorts of research (observation, historical and archival research, content analysis of national media, etc.) and covered a number of problems, including the peculiar nature of the village concerned and the historical and geographic explanations for its cultural isolation, the historical background of the tribunals, the village economic and social structure within which the tribunals operate, the relation of the tribunals to the law of the state (according to which – formally – they are wholly illegal), etc. The central focus is on the functioning of the tribunals themselves: the norms they apply (of which the most important is that a young man must marry a woman who is pregnant by him), their constitution and procedures (they are carried out by the age-group of young, unmarried men who take action after internal consultation and hints or implicit consent from their elders), and the sanctions applied (enforcing promises of marriage; holding offenders up for public display and ridicule). It is a fascinating piece of work, marred only by a certain unclarity of scientific purpose whose explanation lies in the particular history of the project itself and the fact that its inspiration lay in the desire of a group of lawyers to break out of the bounds of traditional legal scholarship and see whether the research techniques of anthropology could enrich their work. Like the Bali-Lombok project, conceived at about the same time by some of the same people, its conception and execution reflect confusion concerning the differences between legal and social scientific research on law. (See Griffiths, 1984b, for an extended discussion of this book.)

At the moment Strijbosch is engaged in research concerning the indigenous law of a small Molluccan community in the Netherlands. The emphasis is on the maintenance in the Netherlands of adat rules and institutions, and the way in which the radically different circumstances of social life in the Netherlands affects their functioning and implications (see Strijbosch, 1982b).

The gradual obliteration of the distinction between the sociology and anthropology of law is beginning to bear fruit in the research projects of the 'sociological' half of the discipline.[28] Thus Hoekema (professor of sociology of law at the University of Amsterdam) is currently responsible for a major study of institutionalized patterns of decision-making in bureaucratic agencies in which the influence of an anthropological approach is evident in several respects. Thus, for example, the object of study is not the aggregate output of such processes, but the processes themselves and the ways in which they are structured by the 'semi-autonomous social fields' within which they take place. In the course of the research, too, Hoekema and his colleagues have had to confront the fact that the received descriptive concepts with respect to decision-making (e.g. 'judicial', 'legal', 'unauthorized discretion') are folk concepts derived from the way in which lawyers (and many sociologists, especially those of a 'functionalist' persuasion) think about how such agencies ought to function, and are therefore unusable for sociological analysis. They have also had to adjust their research technique to fit the nature of their subject matter and the questions being asked about it, so that interviews and direct observation come to play a prominent role. The project has led so far to two very promising interim reports (Aalders, 1984; Knegt, 1984) in which the influence of the social organization of various administrative agencies on their decision-making is the central theme. Both reports emphasize that explicit reliance on the relevant legal texts is rare in such agencies; what counts is a 'law of the office' which has a general relationship to the official law but derives more directly from the demands of local social organization.

Groenendijk (professor of sociology of law in Nijmegen) is engaged in a research project concerning the social effects of the special legal position of aliens. While the project is primarily legal and 'sociological' in orientation, putting the law of the state and its effects conceptually and as research object at center stage, it does reflect an unusually 'anthropological' approach in that the implications of a special egal status will be studied at the level of micro-interactions and in the context of a specific social situation (mass firings). Such an approach to the working of law was self-consciously chosen instead of a more traditionally 'sociological' focus on the perceptions

---

[28]   Apart from the research projects mentioned in the text, Blankenburg's inaugural lecture for the chair in sociology of law at the law faculty of the Free University of Amsterdam (1982) makes extensive use of anthropologicl literature.

and experiences of the affected group or on the aggregate effects of a given legal provision.[29]

Research in Utrecht concerning the functioning of the law on worker participation councils in business concerns has likewise made use of typically anthropological research techniques. Unfortunately, the published results reflect disappointingly little familiarity with the relevant anthropological literature so that they are rather less interesting than they might have been.[30]

The integration with legal anthropology in the above projects seems, so far, more methodological than theoretical, and it remains to be seen to what extent the concepts deployed and the data analysis will make use of and contribute to comparative, 'anthropological' theory. In some other current research projects the integration between sociology and anthropology of law has begun at the other, theoretical end. Several substantial research undertakings in Groningen have from the outset been conceived and carried out within the context of the theory of litigation, a general, comparative theory concerning the behavior of the actors involved in processes of normative conflict, whose provenance is largely 'anthropological' (see Griffiths, 1983b). One project deals with the processes by which divorcing parents arrive at decisions concerning the future of their children (in particular, custody and visitation), another with the use of a new administrative appeals procedure (*Arob bezwaarschriften-procedure*) (see Breeuwsma and others, 1984), and a third with the interaction between lawyers and their clients (see Berends, 1984).

Other publications during the 1970s

Incidental publications in the 1970s by Dutch legal anthropologists, not dealt with above in some more specific context, are as follows:

F. von Benda-Beckmann. In addition to the various products of the research in Minangkabau, F. von Benda-Beckmann has published several articles dealing with problems of comparison in legal anthropology. In "Modern

---

[29] See Groenendijk and others (1982) for an early description of the proposed research.

[30] The first published results of this research are in van den Heuvel (1983), reviewed in Griffiths (1985b).

law and traditional societies'' (1979b) he shows how the opposition between 'modern' and 'traditional' law, which plays such a prominent part in most discussions of 'law and development', is based on a set of misleading assumptions concerning the relationship between law and social change. He illustrates his argument with a marvellously well-taken example of a run-of-the mill inheritance conflict, in which it turns out that although freedom of disposition over self-acquired property is often regarded as one of the hallmarks of 'modern' law, the fact is that 'modern' Dutch law gives far less room for individual freedom of disposition and accords more weight to kinship than does the 'traditional' law of Minangkabau. he also argues – in the same vein as in his article with K. von Benda-Beckmann on legal change in Minangkabau (1981b) – that it is essential when discussing the relationship between legal change and social change to distinguish between a norm and its social function.

In "Anthropology and comparative law" (1981c) he deals with the conceptual problems involved in anthropology as an inherently comparative discipline whose ultimate goal is not idiosyncratic description but "a systematic understanding and explanation of different social conditions in both time and space". "The concepts and categories of the anthropologist's own language are," he observes, "usually unable to meet the requirements of a language of comparison since their meanings are often too strongly bound to a specific culture." He deals, in particular, with the problem of an empirical concept of 'law' itself. His argument is that definitions of law in terms of "norm typology" (a 'legal' norm is a norm whose violation elicits a particular type of 'sanction') are unsuitable both for descriptive and for explanatory purposes because they include as an element of the definition of law a group of factors (concerning the institutional organization for its administration) which there is every reason to suppose are explanatory variables with respect to variation in the manifestations of law. He goes on to show that the common (but misleading) notion that 'traditional' law is less precise and clear than 'modern', western law, and indeed the whole common but misguided opposition between such sorts of law, derives from overemphasis on the supposed typological characteristics of 'law' and a resulting inattention to a number of more fundamental dimensions on which the manifestations of law can vary. The ensuing false comparisons, deriving from the implicit assumption that peculiarly western structural features of law, which are the consequence of particular institutional arrangements, can be regarded as definitional of law in general, stand in the way both of careful analysis of variation within legal systems and of the development of a genuinely comparative theory of law.[31]

In "Some comments on the problems of comparing the relationship of state and traditional systems of justice in Africa and Indonesia" (1981a) he shows how discussion of the impact of (neo-)classical rule on indigenous legal systems has been hampered by the failure to make four essential kinds of distinctions: between the 'use' aspect and the 'efficiency' aspect of legal institutions (the extent to which continuous use is made of them need not correspond with their capacity to dispose definitively of the case brought to them); between different forms of political organization of indigenous societies, in particular the extent to which governmental and judicial functions are functionally and institutionally dispersed; between different state policies toward indigenous institutions (and, as a consequence, different sorts of neo-indigenous institutions) ranging from full incorporation to official elimination; and between interaction between legal institutions on the same level (village; state) and interaction across different levels of socio-political organization. He illustrates the importance of these distinctions and of avoiding sweeping generalizations concerning the relationship between state and indigenous law, with a number of concrete examples.

Finally, in his recent inaugural lecture, "In search of the lesser evil in the jungle of legal pluralism" (1983), he argues that the over-optimism which has plagued discussions of 'development' found its natural expression in the notion of "law as ideal order projected into the future" (1983: 7). The 'causal-deterministic' conception of the relationship between law and its social functions, which is reflected in the 'law and development' literature, and the resulting hostility toward local customary law as a supposed obstacle to development, led to development programs and projects based upon "fascinating ignorance of existing law and fundamental misconceptions of the social significance of law" (1983:3). Von Benda-Beckmann discusses the place of law in society, using arguments derived from his earlier writings, and concludes that non-intervention by the state in existing legal

---

[31]   For an example of the sort of thing von Benda-Beckmann has in mind see Schuyt (1982), discussed by Griffiths (1984c).

arrangements at the local level will generally constitute a lesser evil than the results of interventionism.[32]

K. von Benda-Beckmann discusses the relationship between sociology of law and comparative law in a recent article (1979). She argues that comparative law, in looking for superficial similarities in rules, is often guilty of 'false comparisons' and that attention to the circumstances of law is essential when comparing legal systems.

G. van den Bergh's characteristic contribution to the literature of legal anthropology – leaving aside his research on village tribunals – involves the explorative discussion of a number of conceptual questions which lie at the border between legal history and Roman law on the one hand and anthropology of law on the other. "Legal pluralism and Roman law" (1972) deals with the role which conscious awareness of the fact of legal pluralism has played in modern and ancient legal thought. Van den Bergh begins by observing that legal pluralism is not a doctrinal state of affairs entailing the necessity of choice of an applicable rule of law, but an empirical state of affairs in which different legal orders (which do not necessarily acknowledge each other's legitimacy) are simultaneously effective within a given society. Modern legal thought has no eye for the pluralistic state of affairs in which it is embedded, consumed as it is by the "monistic" conception that 'law' is in its nature unitary and uniform – a conception associated both with western philosophical ideas about law and with the political ideology which accompanied the successful struggle for dominance of the modern nation state.

Legal pluralism was not a practical problem for Roman jurists so long as Roman law itself made no claim to universal, exclusive applicability. The Romans did not interfere with local communities and their law, each tribunal applied its own law, and litigants determined by their selection of a tribunal which law would be applied in their case. When Roman citizenship and its attendant subjection to Roman law was extended to most

---

[32]   See the review of this lecture by Strijbosch (1983b). Other pieces by F. von Benda-Beckmann in the period under discussion include his report to the 11th International Congress on Comparative Law on Dutch scholarship concerning folk property laws and their development (1982b), and an article on "Individualization and criminality" (1982c).

of the inhabitants of the empire, the possibility first presented itself that a Roman citizen before a Roman court might invoke a rule of local, non-Roman law. Nevertheless, little doctrinal attention seems to have been paid to the various questions which a modern lawyer associates with the idea of 'custom' as a source of law (grounds for validity, repugnancy, etc.). The required accommodation to pluralistic reality was apparently made case-by-case and in a pragmatic way. Van den Bergh attributes this relaxed and casuistic approach to the absence, in Roman imperialism, of a "cultural" politics – of a rationalization of political and economic relationships in terms of 'progress'. The conclusion which he draws from this treatment of modern and Roman juridical approaches to legal pluralism is worth quoting:

> The essential point is surely that law has never been unitary and that, however sublime the ideal of justice may be, law itself is a complex of systems of social control situated amidst other complexes of systems of social control. All efforts should certainly be concentrated upon social progress, but what is the use of entering upon the processes of change with irrational monistic preconceptions? (1972: 103)

In "Unity and plurality of law in the modern world" (1975) van den Bergh returns to the 'monistic' blindness to the pluralistic complexity of legal life characteristic of modern legal thought. After a brief consideration of the historical roots of such an ideological preconception, he focusses upon its importance as an implicit basis for theories of development. Notions concerning European legal development have often reappeared in the guise of universal models, put forward as recipes for development in the third world. If we reexamine the monistic conception critically in the light of the actual world around us, however, we are forced to the conclusion that it does little justice to the myriad forms of legal diversity characteristic of modern social reality. A modern state can apparently perfectly well tolerate a high degree of legal pluralism, and "the state which declares that it is the only source of law is like the Baron of Munchhausen, who said he had pulled himself out of the swamp by his own bootstraps" (1975: 25). We have got to rethink the whole idea of legal uniformity and its relevance for development. The question of the importance of uniformity – and for whom it is important – must be asked in concrete social circumstances. Uniformity of law, even going far beyond national boundaries, may be of great importance in some areas of social life (business organization, trade, communications, etc.), and wholly unimportant or positively damaging in others (e.g., family law). Folk law, in turn, can be an instrument of oppression and exploitation which stands in the way of desireable social change, but it can also be the cement of social integration and thus a condition of sound social development.

In "On comparing early and primitive law" (1982) van den Bergh addresses the question: "What is the use of ethnographical materials for the study of early (i.e. Roman and Germanic) law, what is the validity of comparisons, is it possible to fill the gaps in our historical knowledge with anthropological data?" (1982: 168). He concludes that legal anthropology can offer stimulation in the "context of discovery", in which historical theories concerning early law are formulated, and can serve to falsify "generalized assumptions about primitive man" (1982: 181), but cannot provide the legal historican "with facts unknown from our historical sources" (1982: 180).[33]

In "The concept of folk law in historical context" (1985) van den Bergh discusses the history of the concept of 'folk law', and related concepts such as 'unwritten law', 'custom(ary) law', etc., from classical antiquity to the present. His thesis is that these concepts always appear as half of a *pair* of concepts, they are always set off against another sort of 'law' (state law, written law, etc.). The concept of 'folk', or 'customary', law has always been an inverted reflection of the characteristics which prevailing legal theory attributes to the law of the state. It has, in other words, throughout its history been a folk concept whose content is determined not by scientific, descriptive considerations but by the particular concerns and preconceptions of legal thought within the system of state law. In this sense, the whole idea of 'folk law' is a product of the law of the state.

[33] Cf. his dry observation:

> Looking at early Roman law without knowledge of contemporary social anthropology simply means that one is lead unconsciously by antiquated ethnological theories which have grown into commonplace beliefs .... If legal history builds its hypotheses on ... ideas which can be falsified from any textbook of social anthropology, one certainly cannot expect it to contribute much to the advancement of knowledge (1982: 179).

J. Griffiths' writings in the area of legal anthropology during the 1970s dealt largely with problems of descriptive theory. In "The divison of labor in social control" (1984a) he argues that the sociology and anthropology of law are ill-served by what he calls 'taxonomic' conceptions of law in which 'law' is conceived as a species of a larger genus, social control, set off from the rest of the species by a taxonomic characteristic such as 'physical sanctions' or 'political authority' or 'the state'.[34] Griffiths argues for a conception of 'the legal' as a continuous sort of variation which is present in all social control: variation in the degree of specialization involved. Within the context of such a descriptive theory, in which social control is seen not as 'legal' or 'non-legal' but as 'more or less legal', the existing taxonomic definitions of law can all be given a place, and the various traditions of research deriving from them made commensurable and thus cumulative with one another. Finally, Griffiths argues that a non-taxonomic conception of law lends itself to the development of explanatory theory concerning law and social control of the sort advocated by Black (1976).

In "The general theory of litigation – a first step" (1983a) Griffiths draws a variety of loose theoretical strands in the sociological and anthropological literature on litigation together into a coherent descriptive theory which can form the foundations for empirical research concerning litigation.[35] In two important respects, current theoretical notions concerning litigation are shown to be inadequate. First the relationship of the parties to each other is generally implicitly conceived as basically dyadic or triadic: two parties, or two parties and an intervenor of some sort. In fact there are usually far more actors involved (e.g., lawyers; interest groups 'supporting' the parties; etc.), whose behavior cannot be analyzed merely as an extension of that of one of the 'parties', and the 'parties' themselves are often internally heterogenous (e.g., a city government, with its potential conflicts between the legal and the 'line' departments), so that their behavior cannot be analyzed as if it were that of a single, internally harmonious person. Furthermore, the dyadic and triadic models suppose fixed relationships during litigation, while it is common that an actor who is a judge at one stage

---

[34] The argument is a more general form of F. von Benda-Beckmann's critique of 'norm-typological' conceptions of law – more general, because it applies to all of the manifestations of law, not only to rules and other standards.

[35] See pp. for examples of research projects conceived in terms of the theory of litigation.

becomes a party at the next (as, for example, when a conflict within a factory is 'appealed' to a labor court).

The second fundamental inadequacy of most current litigation theory lies in its continuing adherence to the folk-concept of a 'case' (or some derivative notion such as 'dispute' or 'grievance') as the basic unit of analysis for litigation theory. Litigation processes must be conceived and studied in relation to *social structure*, not in relation to *court* (or, more generally, dispute-settlement) structure. Only by doing so can some of the recalcitrant problems of litigation research be overcome. The most important of these is the selection of a 'baseline', that is, the population which is taken to be 100% of the object of investigation. Is it enough, for example, when researching administrative appeals, to begin with those who filed an appeal? or must one go back to all who received a disappointing first decision? or to all who asked for such a decision in the first place (including those who got what they asked for)? or to all who might have asked (whether they actually did or not)? Griffiths argues that none of these conceptions of a (potential) 'case' will ultimately do. Litigation research must in principle begin not with 'cases' but with the *relationship in social structure* out of which a given sort of case might arise. These considerations lead to the judgment that the various current models of litigation careers are simplistic and misleading.

"What is legal pluralism?" (1981a) begins with a discussion of the difficulties for a theory of legal pluralism of the dominance of the ideology of 'legal centralism' – the conviction that "law is and should be the law of the state, and is and should be uniform for all persons, exclusive of all other law, and administered by a single set of state institutions" (1981a: 2). The argument here is similar to van denk Bergh's critique of the 'monistic' conception of law, discussed above. Griffiths adds the observation that one common use of the expression 'legal pluralism' – namely, in connection with the juristic analysis of situations of 'recognition' of existing bodies of 'customary law' in colonial and post-colonial settings – has as such nothing to do with legal pluralism in the empirical sense of a situation in a given social field such that behavior pursuant to more than one legal order occurs. On the contrary, the common lawyers' usage denotes a situation defined in terms of the ideology of legal centralism: it denotes a slightly deviant form of unitary state law. The bulk of the paper discusses a variety of descriptive theories of legal pluralism, all of which are shown to rest sooner or later on legal centralist assumptions, and a variety of descriptive theories of law-in-society (Ehrlich, 1936; Pospisil, 1971; Smith, 1965; Moore, 1973) which, because they conceive of social order pluralistically, afford the basis for theory of legal pluralism. Griffiths concludes that Moore's (1973) model of social order as consisting of a myriad of overlapping "semi-autonomous social fields", each with its own internal legal order, affords the best foundation for the construction of a theory of legal pluralism.[36]

J.F. Holleman contributed an article in 1973 to the *Law and Society Review's* special issue dedicated to Hoebel. Holleman used the occasion to air some reservations concerning overreliance on the 'trouble-case method' in legal anthropology. This method, propagated by Hoebel and exemplified in his work, takes law as consisting of (see, e.g., Pospisil, 1971), or in any case to be studied in terms of, the decisions taken in concrete cases of dispute. Holleman's reservations are four-fold. First, the method overlooks the fact that "voluntary observance of the law is ... its most common form of maintenance", which means that "normal and *trouble-less* practice" must be studied, as well as conflict and dispute (1973: 593). Second, emphasis on *trouble* cases overlooks the important phenomenon of "attested law observance" (*gesteunde naleving*) or "preventive law care" (*preventieve rechtszorg*) – central concepts in the adat-law literature – in which local authorities participate in legal transactions with an eye to assuring their validity, removing legal uncertainty, and reducing the likelihood of future dispute. Third, since the likelihood of conflict is unevenly distributed over the various areas of law, emphasis on trouble-cases will produce a distorted picture of the whole body of law. And fourth, decisions in trouble-case are sometimes less reliable sources of information concerning effective legal rules than the responses given to hypothetical questions, because of the role which extra-judicial considerations (which may well be unknown to the ethnographer) often play in the atypical cases

---

[36]   Griffiths wrote three relevant review articles in the period under review, one (1977) on Emile van Rouveroy van Nieuwaal's *A la Recherche de la Justice* (1977a), one (1984b) on van den Bergh and others (1980) on village justice in the Netherlands, and one (1984c) discussing an inaugural lecture by K. Schuyt (1982) and arguing that sociological theorizing about law cannot afford to ignore the literature in anthropology of law. He also wrote an article arguing for a more anthropological approach to the problem of 'law and development' (1983b).

which lead to conflict in court. Holleman ends his article with a caution against over-enthusiastic projects to unify and codify customary law which, as he observes, by increasing the gap between the law on the books and the law in action, may have the opposite of the intended result and actually contribute to greater legal uncertainty.

F. Strijbosch. In his dissertation *Lawyers and the Study of Folk Law in the Dutch East Indies and in Anglophonic Africa* (1980) Strijbosch describes and compares the way in which two groups of scholars – the adat-law school and the English Restatement of African Law project – collected and presented the rules of Indonesiasn and African indigenous law. The book gives a useful review of these two traditions of scholarship, one on which the section on p. 114 ff. of this essay heavily relies.[37] Strijbosch' assumption that the two projects of reducing the rules of folk law to writing were, as such, 'anthropological' in character because they employed the empirical data-collecting methods of legal anthropologists (1980: 160-61, 166) is, however, not convincing. The questions with which both the adat-law school and the Restatement of African Law project were preoccupied – What is a valid rule of (folk) law? What are the authoritative sources of (folk) law? (Strijbosch, 1980: 173, 178) – are internal *legal* questions. Ter Haar was right that one of the ambitions of the adat-law school had been the creation of a positive legal science of folk-law. His critics did not really disagree with him on this point, but only on the subordinate (but not unimportant) issue of the relevant sources of valid adat law. It was only in the 1970s that Dutch legal anthropology began its definitive break with the legal positivist tendency of the adat-law tradition and self-consciously and wholeheartedly adopted the external stance of an empirical social science.[38]

Strijbosch argues in "Research concerning minority groups in the Netherlands: the perspective from legal anthropology" (1982b), that legal anthropology can play a special role in research concerning the legal position of minority groups by emphasizing the legal conceptions, norms and processes of the groups themselves. He describes the recent development of

[37] Strijbosch (1978) gives a brief account in English of the history, methods and concepts of the adat-law school.
[38] See Emile van Rouveroy van Nieuwaal (1982) and K. von Benda-Beckmann (1981b) for reviews of Strijbosch' dissertation.

the anthropology of western societies, the parallel development in legal anthropology, and some of the few examples of legal anthropological research in the Netherlands (in particular, van den Bergh and others, 1980). Strijbosch argues for more research into the law of non-corporate groups (squatters, minority groups, neighborhoods, etc.)[39], defending the importance of such work with a quotation from Galanter (1981: 34):

> To fulfill our commitment to enlarge justice requires that we embark on research that will illuminate the complex relations between official forums and indigenous law. Such research cannot answer the intractable questions of doing justice, but without it we are less likely to identify the real problems and the real choices that confront us.

The future of anthropology of law in the Netherlands. Summary of recent developments

The past decade was a period of rapid and fundamental transition for Dutch anthropology of law. The situation now is in most respects completely changed from what it was a decade ago: all the leading actors are new; the field lost its historic institutional base in Leiden but gained several new ones; sociology of law suddenly sprouted in most law faculties and, after an initial period of mutual ignorance, the integration of the two traditions is now well underway; the adat-law heritage has not been abandoned, but the scope of the field has been enlarged geographically, theoretically and methodologically far beyond the concern for legal policy and the administration of justice which dominated the work of van Vollenhoven and his successors until well after the second world war. The coming years will need to be a period of consolidation of the intellectual and institutional transformations of the decade just behind us.

While the adat-law school is undoubtedly one of the most important and productive early traditions in legal anthropology, by the beginning of the

---

[39] Strijbosch notes that Dutch sociologists of law have tended to concentrate so exclusively on the law of the state that even the internal law of corporate groups (e.g., the disciplinary law of professional groups) has been largely ignored.

1970s Dutch legal anthropology (with the exception of Holleman, who could with as much justice be claimed by the English) had long ceased to be a factor of significance in the modern development of the field. The past decade saw a burst of activity, and especially a growth of social-scientific professionalism, which is rapidly putting an end to that state of affairs. Of particular importance is the gradual relinquishing of the old ideal of service – the desire to produce results of immediate practical applicability. So long as any social science allows its conceptual apparatus and its research agenda to be dictated by the real or imagined problems of daily politics, it is doomed in the long run to produce no scientific insights fundamentally different from or deeper than those implicit in the political discourse from which it takes its cues.

On the other hand, the continuing importance of the adat-law tradition for modern Dutch legal anthropology is striking. While the classics of that tradition are now in many important respects methodologically and theoretically out of date (the failure of the Bali-Lombok project can be largely ascribed to the failure to recognize how much, scientifically speaking, had changed since the war), it remains a major source of theoretical insight and inspiration for the current generation of anthropological researchers who take legal phenomena as their object of study.

The past decade was not only a period of rapid change and growing professionalism, it was also extraordinarily productive and vital. A handful of scholars – inexperienced, on the whole, and with a weak institutional base – mounted several major research projects, published half a dozen books and a large number of articles, produced a number of films, organized several international conferences and played a key role in the main international institutional developments of the decade. A significant amount of their scientific output was in international languages (German, French and English), so that Dutch legal anthropology can be said actively to have presented itself to the international scientific forum.

The quality of this work was also, on the whole, respectable by international standards, and in several cases the products of recent Dutch legal anthropology compare favorably with the best work being published anywhere. Von Benda-Beckmann's *Property in Social Continuity* (1979a) deserves special mention in this regard, as a major contribution to the international literature.

Despite the common adat-law heritage, no single approach – no Dutch 'school' – has dominated the scene. A small group, who maintain close scientific ties with one another, have approached their subject in a healthy variety of ways. While F. von Benda-Beckmann (1979a) reinstated norms at the center of legal anthropological attention, K. von Benda-Beckmann – in the context of the very same Minangkabau research project – has been producing work squarely within the dispute settlement tradition (1981a, 1981c, 1984b). Emile van Rouveroy van Nieuwaal (1977a) puts institutional interaction at center stage, whereas for Strijbosch 91981a) – and for van Rouveroy himself in another work (1975b) – it is the use of law by individual actors which if focussed upon. If an emerging collective focus can be identified, it consists of the following elements: an emphasis on *norms in practice, in and outside of dispute*, with special attention to the circumstances of *legal pluralism* – heterogenous law located in *semi-autonomous social fields* and the *institutional interaction* and *individual manipulation* made inevitable by such pluralism. The primary focus of study is on the *micro-level* of individual processes and interactions, with special attention to the *dynamic dimension* of the situation (both in the sense of the *transformations* involved in individual cases, and with regard to *change in norms* and in particular their *social functions*). But while concrete, micro-level processes are the most important source of data, the ambition of theoretical analysis is *comparative* and *historical*; this entails particular sensitivity to the problem of *folk concepts* (in particular, the identification of law with the law of the state) and to the danger of *false comparisons* (in particular, the misleading contraposition of 'primitive' and 'modern' law) in the analysis of legal phenomena.

Bibliography:
Current legal anthropological in the Netherlands

J. GRIFFITHS

AALDERS, M.V.C., *Implementatiestijlen in Ambtenarengroepen* [Implementation styles in administrative agencies]. Faculty of Law, Amsterdam, 1984.

ALLOTT, A., G. WOODMAN (eds.), *People's Law and State Law: The Bellagio Papers*. Foris Publications, Dordrecht (forthcoming).

BARKRI-SIGIT, M., F. von BENDA-BECKMANN, The Netherlands Onderzoek Centrum voor het Recht in Zuid-Oost Azië en het Caraïbisch Gebied. *Improving Access to Indonesian Collections in the Netherlands*. Centre for the History of European Expansion, Leiden (1981), 31-32.

BENDA-BECKMANN, F. von, *Rechtspluralismus in Malawi* [Legal pluralism in Malawi]. Weltforum Verlag, München, 1970.

BENDA-BECKMANN, F. von, *Property in Social Continuity: Continuity and Change in the Maintenance of Property Relationships through Time in Minangkabau, West Sumatra*. Martinus Nijhoff, The Hague, 1979a.

BENDA-BECKMANN, F. von, Modernes Recht und traditionelle Gesellschaften [Modern law and traditional societies]. *Verfassung und Recht in Übersee* (1979b) 12, 337-351.

BENDA-BECKMANN, F. von, Some comments on the problems of comparing the relationship between traditional and state systems of administration of justice in Africa and Indonesia. *Journal of Legal Pluralism* (1981a) 19, 165-175.

BENDA-BECKMANN, F. von, Rechtsantropologie in Nederland [Legal Anthropology in the Netherlands]. Special number of *Sociologische*

150

Gids (1981b) 28, 297-400. Edited and with an introduction (id.: 298-304) by F. von Benda-Beckmann.

BENDA-BECKMANN, F. von, Ethnologie und Rechtsvergleichung [Ethnology and comparative law]. *Archiv für Rechts- und Sozialphilosophie* (1981c) 67. An English version will be published in Folk Law Group (n.d.).

BENDA-BECKMANN, F. von, Some comparative generalizations about the differential use of state and folk institutions in dispute settlement. Paper delivered at the Conference of the Commission on Folk Law, Bellagio, 21-25 September 1981d. Forthcoming in *Allott and Woodman*, 1983.

BENDA-BECKMANN, F. von, Ayam gadang toh batalua? Changing Values in Minangkabau property and inheritance law and their relation to structural change. *Indonesia Circle* (1982a) 27, 26-38.

BENDA-BECKMANN, F. von, The development of folk property laws in complex societies: An overview of Dutch scholarship, with special references to the property law of the Minangkabau, West Sumatra. H. Jessurun d'Oliviera (ed.), *Netherlands' Reports to the XIth International Congress of Comparative Law, Caracas, 1982b*. Kluwer, Deventer, 1982b.

BENDA-BEKCMANN, F. von, Individualisierung und Kriminalität – eine rechtsethnologische Betrachtung [Individualization and criminality – a legal anthropological view]. *Zeitschrift für Rechtssoziologie* (1982c) 3, 14-30.

BENDA-BECKMANN, F. von, *Op zoek naar het kleinere euvel en de jungle van het rechtspluralisme* [In search of the lesser evil in the jungle of legal pluralism]. Inaugural lecture, Agriculture University, Wageningen, 24.2.1983.

BENDA-BECKMANN, F. von, Van Vollenhoven over het Adatrecht [Van Vollenhoven on Adat-law]. *Nederlands Juristenblad*, 33 (1984), 1045-1037.

BENDA-BECKMANN, K. von, Einige Bemerkungen über die Beziehung zwischen Rechtssoziologie und Rechtsvergleichung [Some comments on the relationship between sociology of law and comparative law]. *Zeitschrift für Vergleichende Rechtswissenschaft*, 78 (1979), 51-67.

BENDA-BECKMANN, K. von, Forum shopping and shopping forums – dispute settlement in a Minangkabau village in West Sumatra. *Journal of Legal Pluralism* (1981a) 19, 117-159.

BENDA-BECKMANN, K. von, Review of Strijbosch (1980). *NNR* (1981b) 2, 70-74.

BENDA-BECKMANN, K. von, Folk law and state courts in West Sumatra, Indonesias. Paper delivered at the conference of the Commission on Folk Law, Bellagio, 21-25 September 1981. Forthcoming in *Allott and Woodman*, 1983.

BENDA-BECKMANN, K. von, Traditional values in a non-traditional context: Adat and state courts in West Sumatra. *Indonesia Circle* (1982a) 27, 39-50.

BENDA-BECKMANN, K. von, *The Broken Stairways to Consensus: Village Justice and State Courts in Minangkabau*. Foris Publications Dordrecht. Verhandelingen van het Koninklijk Instituut voor Taal-, Land- en Volkenkunde No. 106, 1984a.

BENDA-BECKMANN, K. von, The social significance of Minangkabau State Court Decisions. *Journal of Legal Pluralism*, 23 (1984b). Represented in von Benda-Beckmann, K. (1984b).

BENDA-BECKMANN, K. von, Evidence and legal reasoning in Minangkabau State Courts. *Von Benda-Beckman, K., and Strijbosch*, 1985. Reprinted in Von Benda-Beckmann, K. (1984a).

BENDA-BECKMANN, F. and K. von, Om de taak van den onderzoeker [On the task of the researcher]. *Cornelis van Vollenhoven Stichting* (1975) (1874-1974), 17-21.

BENDA-BECKMANN, F. and K. von, Rechtsspraak in Indonesia [Adjudication in Indonesia]. *Intermediair*, 18 May 1979; reprinted in R. Kamerling (ed.), *Indonesië Toen en Nu. Intermediair*, Amsterdam, 1980, 127-145.

BENDA-BECKMANN, F. and K. von, De zwarte haan vliegt 's nachts [The black rooster flies at night]. *Afscheidsalbum Geert van den Steenhoven*, 1981a, 101-110.

BENDA-BECKMANN, F. and K. von, Rechtsveranderingen in Minangkabau [Legal chanfge in Minangkabau]. *Sociologische Gids* (1981b) 28, 365-390. An expanded English version, first delivered at the Minangkabau Symposium, IUAES Intercongress, Amsterdam, April 1981, entitled "Transformations and change in Indonesian adat", will be published in L.L. Thomas and F. von Benda-Beckmann ;(eds.), *Minangkabau Social, Cultural and Political Forms: Perspectives on*

Continuity and Change. University of Ohio Press, Athens (forthcoming).

BENDA-BECKMANN, K. von, T. STRIJBOSCH, *Essays on Legal pluralism: Anthroplogy of law in the Netherlands.* Foris Publications, Dordrecht, 1985 (forthcoming).

BERENDS, M., *De interactie tussen Advocaten en hun Echtscheidingscliënten* [The interaction between lawyers and their divorce clients]. Faculty of Law, University of Groningen, Groningen, 1984.

BERGH, G.C.J.J. van den, Le pluralisme juridique en droit romain [Legal pluralism in Roman Law]. J. Gillissen (ed.), *Le Pluralisme juridique.* Université de Bruxelles, *Jurist* 4 (n.s.), 1969, 338-350.

BERGH, G.C.J.J. van den, Eenheid en veelheid van recht in de moderne wereld – enkele gedachten over de toekomst van het volksrecht [Unity and diversity in modern law; some thoughts about the future of folk law. *'t Exempel Dwinght – Opstellen aangeboden aan prof. mr. I. Kisch.* Tjeenk Willink, Zwolle (1975), 17-26. An English version will be published in Folk Law Group, n.d.

BERGH, G.C.J.J. van den, On comparison early and primitive law. *Hommage à /Hulde aan/ Tribute to René Dekkers.* Bruyland, Brussels, 1982, 167-185.

BERGH, C.G.J.J. van den, The concept of folk law in historical context. Forthcoming in: *Von Benda-Beckmann, K. and Strijbosch*, (1985).

BERGH, G.C.J.J. van den, et al., *Staphorst en zijn Gerichten* [Staphorst and its popular tribunals]. Boom, Meppel, Amsterdam, 1980. Publications on Folk Law No. 5 – an English summary was published in the same series, and an extensive summary of the findings is given in Griffiths, 1983b.

BINSBERGEN, W. van, Law in the context of Nkoya Society. *Roberts* (1977), 36-68.

BLACK, D., *The Behaviour of Law.* Academic Press, New York, 1976.

BLANKENBURG, E., *Het Idee van een Maatschappij zonder Recht* [The idea of a society without law]. *Inaugural Lecture.* Free University of Amsterdam, 22 January 1982.

BOHANNAN, P., *Justice and Judgment among the Tiv.* Oxford University Press, London, 1957. Revised edition 1968.

BOHANNAN, P., The differing realm of the law. Nader, L. (ed.), The ethnography of Law, *American Anthropologist*, 67 (1965) 6, 33-42 (special publication).

BOHANNAN, P., Ethnography and comparison in Legal anthropology. L. Nader (ed.), *Law in Culture and Society*. Aldine Pub. Co., Chicago, 1969.

BREEUWSMA, C., et al., *Arob Praktijken* [The law on administrative appeals in its practical working]. Kluwer, Deventer, 1984.

COHEN, M., *Het Blijversrecht* [The succession to agricultural property according to local law]. Van der Loeff, Enschede, 1958.

COHEN, M., De evolutie van het blijversrecht in de laatste 12jaar [Changes in local legal practice concerning the succession to agricultural property over the last 12years]. *Plus Est en Vous* (festschrift Pitlo). Tjeenk Willink, Haarlem, 1970, 309-328.

CORNELIS VAN VOLLENHOVEN STICHTING, *Herdenking van de 100ste geboortedag van C. van Vollenhoven* (1874-1974) [Commemoration of the 100th anniversary of the birth of Cornelis van Vollenhoven (1874-1984)]. C. van Vollenhoven Stichting, Leiden, 1975.

EHRLICH, E., *Fundamental Principles of the Sociology of Law* (Moll transl.). Harvard University Press. Cambridge, 1936. First German edition, 1913.

GALANTER, M., Justice in many rooms: Courts, private ordering and indigenous law. *Journal of Legal Pluralism* (1981) 19, 1-47.

GLUCKMAN, M., *The Judicial Process among the Barotse of Northern Rhodesia (Zambia)*. Manchester University Press, Manchester, 1973. First edition, 1995).

GOLDSCHMIDT, J., *National and indigenous constitutional law in Ghana – Their development and their relation to each other*. Dissertation, Faculty of Law, University of Leiden, 1981.

GRIFFITHS, J., Review of Emile van Rouveroy van Nieuwaal (1976). *African Law Studies* (1977), 15, 100-117.

GRIFFITHS, J., *What is legal pluralism/* Paper delivered at the annual meeting of the Law and Society Association, Amherst, Mass., 12-14 June 1981. This is a revised and expanded version of the "The legal integration of minority groups set in the context of legal pluralism". Paper delivered at the conference on "Staatsrecht en minderheidsgroepen", Leiden University, 6 april 1979, and printed in the reader publishe for the conference, 1981a.

GRIFFITHS, J., Four laws of interaction in circumstances of legal pluralism. Paper delivered at the conference of the Commission on Folk Law, Bellagio, 21-25 September 1981b. To be published in *Allott and Woodman*, 1985.

GRIFFITHS, J., The general theory of litigation. A first step. Forthcoming in: *Zeitschrift für Rechtssoziologie*, 1983a.

GRIFFITHS, J., Recht in ontwikkeling [Law and development], 5. *Recht en Kritiek* (1983b), 175-191.

GRIFFITHS, J., The division of labor in social control. Black, D. (ed.), *Towards a General Theory of Social Control* Vol. 1, Academic Press, New York, 1984a, 37-70.

GRIFFITHS, J., Village justice in the Netherlands. Review article on van den Bergh and others (1980). *Journal of Legal Pluralism* 22 (1984b) 17-42, and *Tijdschrift voor Rechtsgeschiedenis*, 52 (1984b) 87.

GRIFFITHS, J., Heeft de rechtssociologie een toegevoegde waarde? [Does the sociology of law have an added value?]. Review of Schuyt, 1982. *Mens en Maatschappij* (1984c) 59, 82-97.

GRIFFITHS, J., *Anthropology of Law in the Netherlands in the 1970s and its historical background*. Forthcoming in von Benda-Beckmann, K., and Strybosch (1985a). An earlier, more exhaustive version is published in: *NNR* (1983) 2, 132-240.

GRIFFITHS, J., Review of van den Heuvel (1983). Forthcoming in: *Rechtsgeleerd Magazijn Themis* (1985b).

GROENENDIJK, K. and others, De sociale betekenis van een afwijkende rechtspositie [The social significance of a deviant legal status]. *NNR* (1982) 2, 73-87.

GULLIVER, P., *Social Control in an African Society – a Study of the Arusha: Agricultural Masai of Northen Tanganyika*. Routledge & Kegan Paul, London, 1963.

GULLIVER, P., *Disputes and Negotiations*, Academic Press, New York, 1979.

HAAR, B. ter, *Het adatprivaatrecht van Nederlandsch-Indië in wetenschap, practijk en onderwijs* [Adat private law of the Netherlands Indies in legal science, legal practice, and legal education]. J.B. Wolters, Groningen/Batavia. Memorial lecture delivered on the 13th anniversary of the founding of the Law School in Batavia, 1937.

HAAR, B. ter, *Beginselen en Stelsel van het Adatrecht* [Principles and system of adat law]. J.B. Wolters, Groningen/Batavia, 1939.

HAAR, B. ter, *Adat Law in Indonesia*. Institute of Pacific Relations, New York, 1948. English version of ter Haar (1939), edited and translated by E. Hoebel and A. Schiller.

HARRELL-BOND, B., U. RIJNSDORP, *Family law in Sierre Leone*. African Studies Centre, Leiden, 1975.

HARRELL-BOND, B., U. RIJNSDORP, *The emergence of the "Stranger-permit" marriage and other new forms of conjugal union in Sierra Leone. Roberts* (1977), 205-223.

HESSELING, G., *Senegal; Staatsrechtelijke en politieke ontwikkelingen* [Senegal; Constitutional and political developments]. Kluwer, Amsterdam, 1982.

HEUVEL, G. van den, *Industrieel burgerschap als uitnodiging; een onderzoek naar de betekenis van medezeggingschapsrecht in de praktijk* [Industrial citizenship as an invitation; research on the meaning of worker participation in law practice]. Kluwer, Deventer, 1983.

HOEBEL, E., *Law of primitive man*. Harvard University Press, Cambridge, 1964.

HOLLEMAN, J., *Shona Customary Law*. Oxford University Press, London, 1952.

HOLLEMAN, J., *Chief, Council and Commissioner*. Van Gorcum, Assen, 1969.

HOLLEMAN, J., Trouble-cases and trouble-less cases in the study of customary law and legal reform. *Law and Society Review* (1973) 7, 585-609. To be reprinted in Folk Law Group, n.d.

HOLLEMAN, J., *Issues in African Law*. Mouton, The Hague, 1974.

HOLLEMAN, J., Some problems of evidence in Shona Tribal Law. Fates, M., S. Patterson (eds.), *Studies in African Social Anthropology*. Academic Press, London (1975a), 75-94.

HOLLEMAN, J., Van Vollenhoven en het Adatrecht [Van Vollenhoven and Adat law]. *C. van Vollenhovenstichting* (1975b), 9-15.

HOLLEMAN, J., Disparities and uncertainties in African law and judicial authority: A Rhodesian case study. *African Law Studies* (1979a) 17, 1-35.

HOLLEMAN, J., Law and anthropology: A necessary partnership for the study of legal change in plural systems. *Journal of African Law* (1979b) 23, 117-130.

HOLLEMAN, J., Volksrecht in Leiden [Folk law in Leiden]. *NNR* (1981a) 2, 17-33.

HOLLEMAN, J., Een lijk op kerstfeest [A corpse at the Christmas celebrations]. *Afscheidsalbum Geert van den Steenhoven* (1981b), 41-52.

HOLLEMAN, J., Editor's Foreword. *Van Vollenhoven* (1981c).

HOOKER, B., *Legal Pluralism: An Introduction to Colonial and Neo-colonial Laws*. Oxford University Press, London, 1975.

KAHN, J., Review of F. von Benda-Beckmann (1979a). *Indonesia Circle*, 22 (1980), 81-88.

KLEI, J. van der, G. HESSELINGS, Anciens et nouveaux droits fonciers chez les Diola au Sénégal et leurs conséquences pour la répartition des terres [Old and new land, law among the Diola in Senegal and their significance for the redistribution of land]. *African Perspectives* (1979) 1, 53-66.

KNEGT, R., *Onregelmatig redelijk; Ambtenaren en de toepassing van de woonruimte- en de bijstandswet* [Irregular but reasonable; public officials and the administration of housing-distribution of land]. Department of Sociology of Law, University of Amsterdam, Amsterdam, 1984.

KOESNOE, M., *Report Concerning a Research of Adat Law on the Islands of Bali and Lombok*, 1971-1973. Institute for Folk Law Nijmegen, Publications on Folk Law No 4, 1977.

KONINGS, P., Capitalist rice-farming and land allocation in Northern Ghana. *Journal of Legal Pluralism*, 23 (1984), 89-119.

KUPER, A., The Kgalagari and the jural consequences of marriage. *Mass.*, 5 (1970a), 466-482.

KUPER, A., *Kalahari village politics; an African democracy*. Cambridge University Press, Cambridge, 1970b.

KUPER, A., Council structure and decision-making. Richards, A., A. Kuper (eds.), *Councils in action*. Cambridge University Press, Cambridge (1971), 80-99.

LETTE, J., Incorporation and ownership. A case of a Bajau fishing village in Sabak, Malaysia. *Essays in Rural Sociology in honour of R.A.J. van Lier*. Department of Rural Sociology, Agricultural University Wageningen, Wageningen (1981), 151-170.

LEV, D., The lady and the banjan tree: Civil law change in Indonesia.

American Journal of Comparative Law (1965) 14, 282-307.

LEV, D., *Islamic Courts in Indonesia*. University of California Press, Berkeley, 1972.

LEV, D., Review of Van Vollenhoven (1981). *Journal of Legal Pluralism*, 22 (1984), 147-155.

MOORE, S., Comparative studies. Nader, L. (ed.), *Law in culture and society*. Aldine Pub. Co., Chicago, 1969.

MOORE, S., Law and anthropology. Siegel, B. (ed.), *Biennal Review of Anthropology 1969*. Standford University Press, Standford, 1970. Reprinted in Moore, 1978.

MOORE, S., Law and social change: The semi-autonomous social field as an appropriate subject of study. *Law and Society Review* (1983) 7, 719-746. Reprinted in Moore, 1978.

Moore, S., *Law as Process: An Anthroplogical Approach*. Routledge & Kegan Paul, London, 1978.

MOORE, S., Review of F. von Benda-Beckmann (1979a). *Journal of Legal Pluralism* (1983) 21, 163-168.

NADER, L., The anthropological study of law. Nader, L. (ed.), The ethnography of law. In: *American Anthropologist*, 67 (1965) 6, part 2 (special publications).

NIGRI, A., La méthode du jurist ethnologique, de l'époque de l'ethnologie juridique de Post à l'époque de la floraison de l'anthropologie culturelle [The method of the legal ethnologist from the time of Post's juridical ethnology to the flourishing of cultural anthropology]. *Italian National Reports to the Xth International Congress on Comparative Law*. Giuffrè, Milan (1978), 37-62.

NEWSLETTER of the Commission on Folk Law and Legal Pluralism of the International Union of Anthropological and Ethnographic Sciences, Institute for Folk Law. Nijmegen, 1969 Vol. I – 1982 Vol. VII.

NEWSLETTER of the Volksrechtkring. Institute for Folk Law, Nijmegen. Appeared twice a year from 1976 to 1981 (in total, 10 numbers). Since 1982, merged with N.N.R.

NNR: Nieuwbrief voor Nederlandstalige rechtsanthropologen, -psychologen en -sociologen. Organ of the Association for the Social-Scientific Study of Law.

OSSENBRUGGEN, F. van, Prof. Mr. Cornelis Van Vollenhoven als ontdekker van het adatrecht [Prof. Cornelis van Vollenhoven as the discoverer of adat-law]. *Bijdragen tot de Taal-, Land- en Volkenkunde van Nederlandsch Indië* (1933) 90, IXLI.

OUDEN, J. den, Changes in land tenure and land use in a Bamileke Chiefdom, Cameroon, 1900-1980: An historical analysis of changes in control over people, land and production. *Essays in Rural Sociology in honor of R.A.J. van Lier*. Department of Rural Sociology, Agricultural University of Wageningen, Wageningen (1981), 172-261.

POSPISIL, L., *Anthropology of Law – A Comparative Theory*. Harper & Row, New York, 1971.

RIJNSDORP, V., Different views about paternal rights in Bo (Sierra Leone), *Law and family in Africa*. Mouton, The Hague, 1977.

ROBERTS, S., *Order and dispute; An introduction to legal anthroplogy* Pinguin books, Harmondsworth, 1979.

ROBERTS, S., Review of F. von Benda-Beckmann, 1979a. *Modern Law Review* (1983) 45, 355-360.

ROUVEROY VAN NIEUWAAL, E. van, Droit coutumier et droit moderne au Togo [Customary law and modern law in Togo]. *Recueil Penant* (1975a) 747, 5-18.

ROUVEROY VAN NIEUWAAL, E. van, The plot of the sophisticated son-in-law; disparity between old and new ways of establishing rights over land in N'zara (Sandanné Mango), North Togo. *Kroniek van Africa* (1975b) 4 47-58. See Emile and Els van Rouveroy van Nieuwaal (1982), for a revised and expanded version.

ROUVEROY VAN NIEUWAAL, E. van, *A la Recherche de la Justice; Quelques Aspects du Droit Matrimonial et de la Justice du Juge de Paix et du Chef Supérieur des Anufòm à Mango dans le Nord du Togo* [In search of justice; some aspects of matrimonial law and of the administration of law by the justice of the peace and by the paramount chief of the Anufòm in Mango, Northern Togo]. African Studies Centre, Leiden, 1977a.

ROUVEROY VAN NIEUWAAL, E. van (cont.), Qui terre a guerre a: la disparité entre la manière coutumière et la manière moderne d'obtenir des droits fonciers à N'Zara dans le Nord du Togo [He who has land has trouble; differences between the customary and modern ways of acquiring land rights in N'Zara, Northern Togo]. *Recueil Penant* (1977b) 756, 149-170.

ROUVEROY VAN NIEUWAAL, E. van, Terre au Nord-Togo: quelques

aspects sur la relation Anufè-Ngam en matière foncière [Land in Northern Togo: Some aspects of the relationship between the Anufòm and the Ngam Ngam in relation to land]. *African Perspectives* (1979) 1, 139-151.

ROUVEROY van NIEUWAAL, E. van, Bases juridiques du droit coutumier au Togo dans l'époque coloniale allemande (1884-1914) [The legal basis of customary law in Togo since the German colonial period]. *Verfassung und Recht in Übersee* (1980a) 13, 27-35.

ROUVEROY van NIEUWAAL, E. van, Chieftaincy in Northern Togo. *Verfassung und Recht in Übersee* (1980b) 13, 115-123.

ROUVEROY VAN NIEUWAAL, E. van. Review of Strijbosch, 1980. *Nederlands Juristenblad* (1982) 57, 110-112.

ROUVEROY VAN NIEUWAAL, E. and E. van, MBAMBIM (film with accompanying explanatory booklet including text; available in Dutch, English and French; 23 mins.). African Studies Centre, Leiden, 1973.

ROUVEROY VAN NIEUWAAL, E. and E. van, SHEREA (film with accompanying explanatory booklet including text; available in Dutch, English and French; 24 mins.). African Studies Centre, Leiden, 1975a.

ROUVEROY VAN NIEUWAAL, E. and E. van, To claim or not to claim: Changing ideas about the restitution of marital payments among the Anufòm in North Togo. *African Law Studies* (1975b) 12, 100-118. Reprinted in Roberts, 1977.

ROUVEROY VAN NIEUWAAL, E. and E. van, *Ti Anufò, un coup d'oeil sur la société des Anufòm au Nord-Togo* [Ti Anufò, a short account of the society of the Anufom in Northern Togo]. African Studies Centre, Leiden, 1976.

ROUVEROY VAN NIEUWAAL, E. and E. van, A TOAD IN THE COURTYARD (film with accompanying explanatory booklet including text; available in Dutch, English and French; 25 mins.). African Studies Centre, Leiden, 1979.

ROUVEROY VAN NIEUWAAL, E. and E. van, BEKOINDINTU (film with accompanying explanatory booklet including text; available in Dutch, English and French; 32 mins.). African Studies Centre Leiden, 1980.

ROUVEROY VAN NIEUWAAL, E. and E. van, IN SEARCH OF JUSTICE (film with accompanying explanatory booklet including text; available in Dutch, English and French; 52 mins.). African Studies Centre, Leiden, 1981a.

ROUVEROY VAN NIEUWAAL, E. and E. van, Het mogelijke en onmogelijke in verzoening bij Anufòm in Noord-Togo (West-Afrika) [Possibilities and impossibilities of reconciliation among the Anufòm of Northern Togo (West-Africa)] *Scoiologische Gids* (1981b) 28, 305-326.

ROUVEROY VAN NIEUWAAL, E. and E. van, The plot of the sophisticated son-in-law: Old and new ways of establishing rights over land in N'Zara (North Togo). In French: *Droit et Cultures* (1982) 4, 49-70. Forthcoming in English in Folk Law Group, n.d. Revised and expanded version of Emile van Rouveroy van Nieuwaal, 1975b.

ROUVEROY VAN NIEUWAAL, E. van, A.K. AMEGA (eds.), La réforme agro-confière dans les pays du conseil d'entente en Afrique de l'ouest [Agricultural land-law reform in the countries of the Conseil de l'Entente in West Africa]. Special number of *African Perspectives*, 1979.

SCHOTT, R., Main trends in German ethnological jurisprudence and legal ethnology. *Journal of Legal Pluralism* (1982) 20, 37-68.

SCHUYT, C., *Ongeregeldheden – Naar een Theorie van Wetgeving in de Verzorgingsstaat* [The disorder of modern life; toward a theory of legislation in the welfare state]. Inaugural lecture, Samson, Alphen a/d Rijn, 11 juni 1982.

SLAATS, H., K. PORTIER, *Grondenrecht en Zijn Verwerkelijking in de Karo Batakse Dorpssamenleving* [Land law and its application in Karo Batak village society]. Institute for Folk Law Nijmegen, 2 vols. Publications on Folk Law No. 9, 1981a.

SLAATS, H., K. PORTIER, Verwerkelijking van adatrecht in de Karo Batakse samenleving (Indonesië) [Application of adat-law among the Karo Batak (Indonesia)]. *Sociologische Gids* (1981b) 28, 347-364.

SLAATS, H., K. PORTIER, Some notes on administering justice in Karoland, North Sumatra, Indonesia. Smith Kipp, R., R. Kipp (eds.), *Beyond samosir: Recent studies of the Batak peoples of Sumatra*. Papers in International Studies Southeast Asia Series No. 62. Athens, Ohio, 1983.

SMITH, M., The sociological framework of law. H. Kuper, L. Kuper (eds.), *African Law: Adaptation and Development*. University of California Press, Berkeley (1965), 24-28.

SNYDER, F., Anthropology, dispute processes and law. *British Journal of Law and Society*, 8 (1981a), 141-180.

SNYDER, F., Review of van Rouveroy van Nieuwaal and Amèga (1979). *Journal of Legal Pluralism*, 20 (1982), 151-153.

SONIUS, H., *Over mr. Cornelis Van Vollenhoven en het Adatrecht van Indonesië* [On Cornelis van Vollenhoven and the adat-law of Indonesia]. Institute for Folk Law Nijmegen, Publications on Folk Law No. 1, 1976. A translated and abridged version appears as the Introduction to van Vollenhoven, 1981.

SONIUS, H., *Binnenlands Bestuur en Agrarisch Recht in Nederlands-Indië* [Colonial Administration and agrarian law in the Netherlands Indies]. Institute for Folk Law, Publications on Folk Law No. 8, Nijmegen, 1980.

STEENHOVEN, G. van den, *Leadership and law among the Eskimos of the Reservation District, Northern Territories.* Uitgeverij Excelsior, Rijswijk, 1962.

STEENHOVEN, G. van den, *The Land of Kerenda.* Institute for Folk Law, publications on Adat Law No. 5, Nijmegen, 1970.

STEENHOVEN, G. van den, Musjawarah in Karo-land. *Law and Society Review* (1973), 693-718.

STRIJBOSCH, A., Methods and theories of Dutch juridical-ethnological research in the period 1900 to 1977. H. Jessurun d'Oliveira (ed.), *Netherlands Reports to the 10th International Congress of Comparative Law.* Kluwer, Deventer (1978), 1-15.

STRIJBOSCH, A., *Juristen en de Studie van Volksrecht in Nederlands-Indië en Anglofoon Afrika* [Lawyers and the study of folk law in the Netherlands Indies and in Anglophonic Africa]. Institute for Folk Law, publications on Folk Law No. 7, Nijmegen, 1980.

STRIJBOSCH, A., Krediethandelingen op het eiland Lombok [Credit contracts on the Island of Lombok]. *Sociologische Gids* (1981a) 28, 327-346. Forthcoming in English in: K. von Benda-Beckmann and Strijbosch, *Credit contracts on the island of Lombok*, 1985.

STRIJBOSCH, A., Recognition of folk institutions for dispute settlement in Lombok, Indonesia. Paper delivered at the Conference of the Commission on Folk Law, Bellagio, 21-25 September 1981b. Forthcoming in *Allott and Woodman*, 1984.

STRIJBOSCH, A., Onderzoek bij minderheden in Nederland: een rechtsantropologische visie [Research among minority groups in the Netherlands; a legal-anthropological perspective]. *NNR* (1982) 2, 88-104.

STRIJBOSCH, A., De oraties van E. Blankenburg en F. von Benda-Beckmann gezien als tijdverschijnselen [The inaugural lectures of E. Blankenburg and F. von Benda-Beckman as signs of the times]. *NNR* (1983) 1, 23-37.

SYPKENS-SMIT, M., *Land-leenrelaties in de Basse-Casamance (Senegal)* [Land-loan relationships in the Basse-Casamance (Senegal)]. Department of Anthropology, University of Utrecht, Utrecht, 1976 (Student research report).

VERLINDEN, J., L'ethnologie juridique en Belgique de Post à Levi-Strauss [Legal ethnology in Belgium from Post to Levi-Strauss]. *Rapports Belges au 9e Congrès International de Droit Compare, Bruylant, Brussels, 1978, 1-9.*

VOLLENHOVEN, C. van, *Exacte rechtswetenschap [Exact legal science]. Inaugural lecture, Leiden University. Reprinted in: Verspreide Geschriften* Vol. I, 1934. Tjeenk Willing, Haarlem (1901), 3-21.

VOLLENHOVEN, C. van, *Miskenningen van het Adatrecht.* Wrong ideas about adat-law]. Brill, Leiden, 1909.

VOLLENHOVEN, C. van, *The study of Indonesian customary law. Illinois Law Review* (1918) 13. Reprinted in van Vollenhoven, 1933, Vol. III.

VOLLENHOVEN, C. van, *Het Adatrecht van Nederlandsch Indië* [The adat-law of the Netherlands Indies]. (3 vols.). Brill, Leiden, 1918, 1931, 1933.

VOLLENHOVEN, C. van, Families of Language and families of law. *Illinois Law Review* (1921) 15. Reprinted in: *Verspreide Geschriften* Vol. I. Tjeenk Willink, Haarlem, 1934. The original Dutch version, "Taalfamilies en rechtsfamilies", is also reprinted in: *Verspreide Geschriften*, 51-56.

VOLLENHOVEN, C. van, *La Découverte du Droit Indonésien* [The discovery of Indonesian law]. Paris (transl. by N. Pernot) of *De Ontdekking van het Adatrecht.* Brill, Leiden, 1928.

VOLLENHOVEN, C. van, *Van Vollenhoven on Indonesian Adat Law*, J. Holleman (ed.). Nijhoff, The Hague, 1981.